PACTS & TREATIES

HUMAN RIGHTS

SUSAN DUDLEY GOLD

TWENTY-FIRST CENTURY BOOKS
A Division of Henry Holt and Company
New York

Dedicated to James and Louise Thomas, who, by their lives and actions, teach that all humans are entitled to be treated with respect and dignity

Twenty-First Century Books
A Division of Henry Holt and Company, Inc.
115 West 18th Street
New York, NY 10011

Henry Holt® and colophon are trademarks of
Henry Holt and Company, Inc.
Publishers since 1866

Published in Canada by Fitzhenry & Whiteside Ltd.
195 Allstate Parkway, Markham, Ontario, L3R 4T8

Library of Congress Cataloging-in-Publication Data
Gold, Susan Dudley
Human rights / Susan Dudley Gold. — 1st ed.
p. cm. — (Pacts & treaties)
Includes bibliographical references and index.
Summary: Discusses pacts and treaties, both past and present, designed to protect human rights throughout the world, including the League of Nations, and the Geneva Conventions of 1864, 1906, 1929, and 1949.
1. Victims of war—Legal status, laws, etc.—Juvenile literature. 2. Prisoners of war—Legal status, laws, etc.—Juvenile literature. 3. War—Relief of sick and wounded—Juvenile literature. 4. War—Protection of civilians—Juvenile literature. [1. Human rights.]
I. Title. II. Series.
JX5136.G65   1997
341.4'81—dc21   96–40952
                                                                      CIP
                                                                       AC

Photo Credits
Cover illustration and illustrations on pages 12 and 30 © 1996 North Wind Picture Archives.
Illustrations on pages 17 and 27 credited to American Red Cross.
Photographs on pages 35, 47, 52, 59, 61, 64, 69, 79, 82, and 93 credited to UPI/Corbis-Bettmann.
Photographs on pages 40, 56, 67, and 72 credited to Corbis-Bettmann.
Photographs on pages 90 and 101 credited to AFP/Corbis-Bettmann.
Maps on pages 15, 24, 38, 43, 97, and 99 © 1996 Susan D. Gold.

Design, Typesetting, and Layout
Custom Communications

ISBN 0-8050-4811-1
First Edition 1997

Printed in Mexico
All first editions are printed on acid-free paper ∞.
10 9 8 7 6 5 4 3 2 1

13.25

CONTENTS

INTRODUCTION

WORDS AGAINST VIOLENCE

One thousand armed rebels attack a refugee village where the families of their enemies have sought shelter. Wielding machetes and clubs, they hack at the cowering women and children who beg for their lives. More than three hundred people die in the slaughter.

War deprives people of the basic rights to which they are entitled as humans. "Peace is the underlying condition for the full observance of human rights and war is their negation,"[1] the delegates gathered at the 1968 International Conference on Human Rights in Tehran stated in a resolution they adopted there.

But even where there is no war, violence works its evil. Inside a dark cell, men with chains beat an old woman until she can no longer walk. A man is confined to a mental institution because his poem criticized his government. Mothers wander the streets, holding posters showing the faces of their teenage children snatched from their homes in the night by government thugs.

Fighting these outrages with words might seem a futile gesture. But words have been, and continue to be, the primary weapon in the battle for human rights. The

5

words in the treaties, pacts, and declarations, signed by the nations of the world, specify the rights to which all humans, are entitled. They provide the moral compass by which we judge our activities and those of all nations. They set a standard that calls for us to respect life and to maintain the dignity of our fellow human beings, even during war.

The U.S. Constitution and the Bill of Rights, the French Declaration of the Rights of Man, the Soviet Constitution, and the United Nations' Universal Declaration of Human Rights all revolve around the premise that each person, because he or she is human, is entitled to certain rights: to life, free thought and speech, shelter, and food; the right to practice his or her religion; the right to be treated humanely, not to be tortured, killed, or terrorized. These rights are inalienable; that is, each person is born with rights that cannot be taken away by government or law.

Words, of course, can be ignored. With all these written safeguards in place, people are still massacred, men and women are tortured, children are kidnapped and killed. Of what use are these documents? Are they just paper fortresses against the blaze of violence that engulfs the world?

Let's look at the record. In the 1800s, as in other centuries, brutal wars robbed young men of their lives. Swiss businessman J. Henri Dunant's graphic description of the plight of wounded soldiers during the war between Italy and Austria shook the world. In Dunant's skilled words, enemy and allied soldier alike became living, suffering human beings—not just pieces in an army. Dunant and his supporters helped negotiate the Geneva Convention, the first international treaty that sought to guarantee human rights to wounded soldiers.

Dunant's words also helped establish the International Committee of the Red Cross and Red Cross societies throughout the world, which provide care and sustenance for millions of victims of wars and disasters.

Each war has spawned new ways to abuse human beings. But after each war, delegates have met to forge new agreements to extend protections to victims. After the naval wars of the last half of the nineteenth century, a second Geneva Convention expanded protection to those shipwrecked or wounded in maritime battles. Abuse of prisoners of war during World Wars I and II led the Geneva delegates to draw up new conventions regulating their treatment. Adolf Hitler's slaughter and torture of civilians led to a separate treaty on their rights.

Nearly every nation in the world today has signed or acceded (agreed to be a party) to the Geneva Conventions. Although war abuses continue, the treaties have done much to improve the lot of victims of war. According to the Red Cross, millions of people "have been spared much needless misery, degradation, and suffering in wartime, and . . . uncounted numbers of lives have been saved because of the existence of the Geneva Conventions."[2]

Although war magnifies human rights abuses, such abuses take place during peacetime as well. The United Nations, in its Universal Declaration of Human Rights, laid out the rights of individual citizens in everyday life. Like the Geneva Conventions, the Declaration contains only words—there are no means of enforcing the provisions. Eleanor Roosevelt, who headed the commission that drafted the declaration, noted that the document "has no legal value," but she added that it "should carry moral weight."[3]

Continuing its push for human rights, the United Nations has developed more than twenty treaties, or covenants, guaranteeing rights for women and children; political rights; freedom from genocide and racial discrimination; and economic, social, and cultural rights. None have been ratified by all the nations of the world (the United States has not yet ratified the Covenant on Economic, Social, and Cultural Rights or the Convention on the Political Rights of Women). Nevertheless, the covenants set a standard for the nations of the world. When a nation violates the standard, other nations can apply pressure to end the abuses. Economic sanctions and other measures applied to South Africa eventually forced that nation to end apartheid, which promoted widespread discrimination against black citizens and deprived them of their right to vote.

Private organizations have also applied the standards set in international pacts and treaties against violators of human rights. By publicizing abuses, Amnesty International and other human rights groups have been able to exert international pressure on repressive governments. In many cases, political prisoners have been released as a result of their efforts.

The battle has not been won. Torture, murder, and terrorism continue in the world. But in the pages of the world's covenants, in the articles of the Geneva Conventions and the human rights treaties, the goal exists for all to see. Helen Keller described her joy after reading the Braille version of the Declaration of Human Rights: "My soul stood erect, exultant, envisioning a new world where the light of justice for every individual will be unclouded."[4] It is a vision we all can share.

HOW TREATIES WORK

Treaties are agreements made between nations. They may settle boundary disputes, transfer titles of property, make peace, resolve disputes, set up alliances, or agree to handle a particular issue in a certain way (for example, treatment of victims of war). Nations signed the first international agreement on human rights in Geneva, Switzerland, in 1864. This first Geneva Convention set down the rights of wounded and sick soldiers. Additional conventions protected the rights of prisoners of war, those involved in maritime warfare, and civilians during war.

It may take months, sometimes years, for delegates, representing the world's nations, to agree on the exact wording in a treaty. These delegates meet, thrash out their differences, and, finally, agree to sign a declaration or treaty. After the signing, delegates take the document home to get their nations to ratify, or approve, it.

For the United States and other nations, signing a pact is much simpler than ratifying it. Leaders, reluctant to put limits on their nation's power, may refuse to ratify a treaty that gives an international body the right to supervise the behavior of individual nations. Battles between political parties within a country may interfere with ratification. Also a nation may decide not to support a pact if an enemy nation would benefit from it, even if their own nation would benefit as well.

The U.S. Constitution gives the president the power to make treaties with the "advice and consent" of the Senate. For a treaty to be valid, two-thirds of the members present in the Senate must ratify it. The House of Representatives plays no role in approving treaties, but it can block a treaty if it requires a monetary payment, which must be approved by the House.

Once a treaty has been ratified by enough countries, it goes into effect. By ratifying it, nations agree to abide by its terms. Many nations adopt the basic terms of the treaty into their own national code of laws. Today if nations violate the terms, they can be subject to international pressure. In some cases, other nations may agree not to trade with the offender, withdraw their ambassadors, and discontinue foreign aid. If violations are severe, the United Nations may send in its forces to keep the peace or to enforce the treaty (for example, to prevent one nation from invading another).

The United Nations has taken on the task of establishing human rights standards for the world. Its Universal Declaration of Human Rights, adopted in 1948 and signed by almost all the nations of the world, sets forth in thirty principles the rights due all people. The declaration, although not binding, serves as a goal toward which nations should strive to ensure human rights for their citizens and the citizens of the world.

The United Nations has had less success in gaining international support for peacetime treaties, or covenants. Convincing nations to agree to abide by a human rights code during wartime has proven easier than getting them to commit to similar rules for peacetime. Nations have a real interest in protecting their wounded soldiers and unarmed civilians from the ravages of war. In peacetime, however, nations tend to resent international scrutiny of the way they treat the citizens within their own borders. Although most nations agree that people have certain rights, it has been difficult to reach an agreement on exactly what those rights are.

In the case of the human rights treaties, U.S. delegates have frequently approved a pact only to have the president or the Senate or both refuse to ratify it. If too many nations refuse to ratify, the treaty may not go into effect. But, as in the case of many UN treaties, the documents—even those not ratified—effectively put nations on notice that human rights is an international concern. If nations violate the rights of their citizens, the world will take note.

Red Cross workers tend to soldiers wounded during the Austro-Prussian War in 1866.

One

A Businessman's Mission

The people of Lombardy, a northern province of Italy, cheered loudly as Victor-Emmanuel II, the king of Sardinia and Piedmont, boldly led his army through the crowded streets of Brescia. Italy was at war once again.

For three and a half centuries, the nations of Europe had battled over the Mediterranean country, parceling its territories among themselves. Now, in the spring of 1859, Austria, which controlled the northern Italian states of Lombardy and Venetia, had declared war on Italy. Victor-Emmanuel II, who ruled the independent Italian states of Sardinia and Piedmont, sought to drive the Austrians from their strongholds and reunite the divided nation. To strengthen his hand, the king had formed an alliance with Napoleon III, emperor of France.

Napoleon III, the nephew of Napoleon Bonaparte, and his army soon joined the Sardinian forces in Brescia.

Again, the townspeople turned out to show their support of the soldiers they hoped would liberate them. Altogether, 150,000 men gathered in the farmlands surrounding Brescia, hauling an arsenal of four hundred artillery pieces along with them.

The Austrians had retreated to the east, concentrating their forces in a triangle of land bounded on the east by the Mincio River and on the west by the Adige River. Early on the evening of June 23, the 170,000 men of the Austrian army corps began an all-night march to Solferino, a small town about twenty miles southwest of Brescia. In the hours before dawn, they positioned their five hundred pieces of artillery along the low hills that overlooked the Solferino countryside.

Not long after midnight on June 24, the French and Sardinian troops began to move across the Chiese River east of Brescia and march toward Solferino. Both armies, miscalculating the movements of their enemy, planned to camp near Solferino for a day of rest before engaging in battle.

Just outside the town of Castiglione, in the fields of the little town of Solferino, Napoleon's forces found themselves face-to-face with Austrian cannons. This was wine country, where in peaceful times farmers had grown grapes. Now the fields were overgrown with grape vines and mulberry trees. The French soldiers, exhausted from their early-morning march and with only a swallow or two of coffee to ward off hunger, hacked their way through the thickets toward the low hills where the Austrians waited. Their horses stumbled in the dried-up ditches once used to irrigate the crops. Walls three to five feet high,

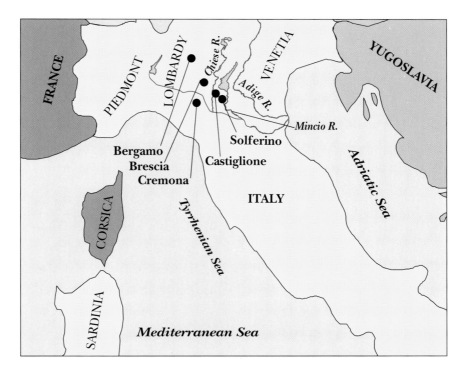

Napoleon's forces and those of the Austrians clashed just outside the town of Castiglione in the northern part of Italy.

along which the grape vines grew, further blocked the way. The cavalry urged their horses over the walls, while those on foot scaled the barriers or found their way around them.

The Austrians were not much better prepared for battle. They had received only a double ration of brandy since beginning their trek the previous evening. Seeing the French soldiers heading for their bunker, they hurriedly prepared their cannons and formed into lines, their white uniforms bright against the green of the hills.

By 6 A.M., the explosive sound of gunfire shattered the

stillness of the country dawn as 320,000 men faced one another, firing guns and cannons along a ten-mile stretch. Tight units of French soldiers marched into the steady fire of Austrian cannons and rifles. As they fell, other soldiers took their place.

Spectators from nearby towns could barely see the action through the haze of smoke and dust: here, a flash of the Austrians' yellow-and-black battle flags, emblazoned with the German Imperial Eagle; there, the sun glinting off the armor of the French Dragoons. Those watching found it hard to breathe in the oppressive June heat, made even more intolerable by the fumes of the guns, the smell of blood and sweat, and the thick dust that arose from the horses' pounding hooves. The noise was almost unbearable. Rifles cracked the air, cannons boomed, men cursed and shouted. Everywhere wounded soldiers could be heard crying, begging for help, pleading for water or for something to ease the pain.

The fighting was fierce. "Here is a hand-to-hand struggle in all its horror and frightfulness," wrote J. Henri Dunant, a young Swiss businessman who witnessed the battle. "Austrians and Allies trampling each other under foot, killing one another on piles of bleeding corpses, felling their enemies with their rifle butts, crushing skulls, ripping bellies open with sabre and bayonet. . . . When they have no weapon left, they seize their enemies by the throat and tear them with their teeth."[1]

The ferocity of the battle took its toll on both sides. Thousands of wounded men lay dying in the fields and hills. Dunant continues with his description of the devastation: "Every mound, every height, every rocky crag, is

J. Henri Dunant was a successful, young businessman from Switzerland, who witnessed the shocking treatment of wounded soldiers at the Battle of Solferino. His book on the subject led to the founding of the International Red Cross Committee and the Geneva Conventions.

the scene of a fight to the death; bodies lie in heaps on the hills and in the valleys."[2] In the chaos of battle, the wagons hauling artillery ran over wounded soldiers unable to get out of the way. In his vivid description, Dunant doesn't flinch from recounting even the goriest scene: "Brains spurt under the wheels, limbs are broken and torn, bodies mutilated past recognition—the soil is literally puddled with blood, and the plain littered with human remains."[3]

One wounded French officer was carried to a nearby chapel, where local residents treated his wounds. When the Austrian forces overtook the area where the chapel was located, a group of Croatian soldiers—allies of the Austrians—broke down the door and crushed the officer's skull with rocks. Other atrocities occurred on both sides.

Field hospitals were set up in every available farmhouse and cottage along the battle site. Black flags indicated where the hospitals were located, to protect them from enemy fire. But the shells continued to pound the sites, fired by soldiers either unaware of their existence in the thick smoke or unwilling to grant them amnesty. Surgeons worked for twenty-four hours straight, often forced to amputate arms and legs without a painkiller of any sort.

Most of the wounded lay where they fell, unable to make it to a hospital. Bullets struck ambulance drivers who tried to move the most seriously wounded. Following the lead of English nurse Florence Nightingale, who had cared for dying soldiers during the Crimean War, canteen women braved the shells and grapeshot to bring water to wounded soldiers in the field. Many of them, too, were shot down as they carried their canteens to the men.

For fifteen hours, the battle raged. A summer storm swept the battlefield in late afternoon. Thunder played a loud accompaniment to the battle sounds as cold rain drenched the weary combatants. A fierce wind whipped up dirt and debris and scattered it along the battle lines. Finally, the Austrians retreated across the Mincio River. Sporadic fighting continued through the night, but the main battle had ended. The French and Italian soldiers had gained control of Lombardy.

When the incessant firing ended at last, the moans of thousands of men could be heard. The fierce battle had left forty thousand soldiers—Austrian, French, Italian, and their allies—dead or wounded on the fields of Solferino. Many of them were not yet twenty years old. It took local citizens and the army three days and three nights to bury the dead. More than one wounded soldier, mistaken for dead, was tossed into the common, un-marked graves.

Throughout the night and all the next day, wagons carried piles of injured soldiers to temporary first-aid sta-tions set up in the nearby towns. Those still left in the field at daybreak had been without food or water for more than twenty-four hours. Desperate to quench their thirst, some drank from the pools of bloody rainwater that dotted the once-green fields. Others begged to be put out of their misery. Many died from hunger and ex-haustion before they could be moved from the field. Sol-diers with only minor wounds developed infections that required their legs or arms to be amputated; still others died from diseases rampant in the dirty, germ-laden fields where they lay.

ORGANIZING A RELIEF EFFORT

The first stop for many of the wounded was Castiglione, the small Italian town where J. Henri Dunant had arrived a few days before to discuss a business deal. At thirty-one, Dunant was well on his way to developing a promising business career. The Geneva bank where Dunant had received his training had appointed him general manager of a subsidiary bank in Algeria when he was still in his twenties. Later, he left the bank and set up his own business.

The young businessman also had success on the international level in his volunteer work. He helped establish a Young Men's Christian Union in his native Switzerland, following the lead of organizers in England and in other countries. At an international conference in Paris in 1855, Dunant led the effort to unite the national groups into a worldwide organization known as the Young Men's Christian Association.

Now, amid almost incomprehensible human suffering, Henri Dunant's business mission gave way to his charitable instincts. While the battle was still being fought, he recruited local women to help him care for the wounded being brought into the town. By the end of the day after the battle, Castiglione, a town of 5,300 residents, was completely overrun with wounded and dying soldiers. Every building was filled with them. The streets were clogged with wagonloads of injured men, brought to town every fifteen minutes. When no more space could be found inside, townspeople laid soldiers on beds of straw under temporary wooden shelters or cloth awnings to protect them from the sun.

At first, some of the volunteers cared only for the French and Italian soldiers. But when they saw Dunant helping anyone in need, they soon followed his example. *Sono tutti fratelli* ("all men are brothers") the Italian women murmured as they bathed the wounds of Austrian soldiers, held the hand of a dying Frenchman, and helped a Croatian sip water through parched lips.

It was nasty work. Flies swarmed around infested wounds; soldiers died in their own filth; men cried out in agony, begging for a doctor. It seemed that the wounded would never stop arriving. Volunteers, although willing, often had no idea what they should do. Others worked until exhaustion forced them to go home and rest. The volunteers soon used up every linen bandage they could find in the town. Dunant sent to surrounding towns for more medical supplies, food, and drink.

Under Dunant's directions, boys filled containers with water and gave tea and soup to those who could drink it. He "practically by force" convinced two curious English tourists, who had stopped by a church to see what was going on, to help care for the wounded soldiers housed there. An Italian priest, a Paris journalist, a merchant, a captured German surgeon, and three Austrian doctors were among other volunteers who lent their help to the wounded of Solferino.[4]

The French soldiers called Dunant the White Gentleman because he was dressed in white as a way to combat the heat. Later, recalling the scene, Dunant described an old sergeant who, "with cold bitterness," told Dunant that he might have survived his wounds if they had been tended sooner. "Now," the soldier said, "by evening I shall be dead!"[5] And he was.

As the days passed, convoys of wounded soldiers traveled to Brescia. There they were treated in the larger town's hospital, schools, and other public buildings, where volunteers had erected fifteen thousand beds. Women in villages along the convoy route treated the soldiers' wounds and fed them soup and lemonade. By this time, doctors from throughout Europe had begun arriving in Brescia and other towns to treat the wounded. Members of relief services in Bergamo and Cremona— large towns south of Brescia—and ladies' auxiliary committees accepted donations for the soldiers, stocked needed supplies, and helped provide care. Gradually, life returned to normal.

Dunant, however, would never again be able to return to business as usual. The image of the wounded and dying soldiers in Solferino haunted him. "You feel sometimes that your heart is suddenly breaking," he related. "It is as if you were stricken all at once with a sense of bitter and irresistible sadness."[6] Driven by "the moral sense of the importance of human life,"[7] the young Swiss businessman decided to do what he could to spare victims of other battles unnecessary suffering.

GENEVA CONVENTION OF 1864

Three years after the battle of Solferino, Henri

Dunant published *Un Souvenir de Solférino* (A Memory of Solferino). In it, he gave a powerful and graphic account of the horrors of the battle and the intense suffering of the wounded. Dunant also proposed the formation of relief societies in the nations of the world that would train volunteers in peacetime to aid and assist the wounded in war.

He called on the leaders of the world to prepare and sign an international convention, or treaty, that would establish the relief societies before another war broke out. "In an age when we hear so much of progress and civilization, is it not a matter of urgency, since unhappily we cannot always avoid wars, to press forward in a human and truly civilized spirit the attempt to prevent, or at least to alleviate, the horrors of war?" Dunant asked his readers. "Humanity and civilization call imperiously for such an organization."[8]

Almost overnight, the small book's vivid images evoked responses from people across Europe. Advances in science and technology had improved the standard of living of many Europeans during the nineteenth century. This new middle class had adopted the humanitarian philosophies espoused by the authors of the U.S. and French constitutions and others that placed high value on individual lives. Henri Dunant's proposals, they agreed, were both humane and practical.

Another consideration strengthened support for Dunant's suggestions. Warfare had changed since the days of knights and kings. The revolutions in the United States and in France had fostered a belief in the equality of people that had spread to the battlefield. Now, soldiers

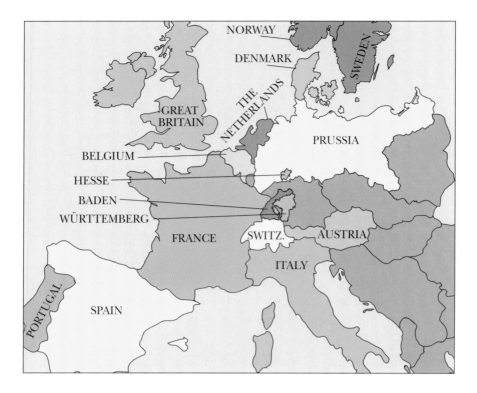

Fifteen European countries sent delegates to the Geneva Conference in August 1864. The nations participating were Baden, Belgium, Denmark, France, Hesse, Italy, the Netherlands, Portugal, Prussia, Spain, Switzerland, Sweden and Norway (one nation until 1905), Great Britain, Austria, and Württemberg. The United States sent a representative but did not participate officially in the conference.

came from all walks of life. This greatly increased the number of soldiers available to fight. At the same time, advances in science had resulted in new, more efficient weapons that could kill or maim large numbers of people. On the battlefield, more soldiers were fighting and dying than ever before.

Soon Dunant was meeting with heads of state throughout Europe, winning support for his ideas wherever he spoke. In February 1863, his home city of Geneva appointed him to a committee to begin the task of organizing relief societies. Serving with Dunant on the committee were Gustave Moynier, president of the Geneva Society of Public Welfare; General G. H. Dufour, who served as president of the committee; and two Swiss doctors, Théodore Maunoir and Louis Appia. The Committee of Five, which would one day develop into the International Committee of the Red Cross, asked Geneva to convene an international conference on the subject.

Responding to Dunant's invitation, thirty-six delegates from fourteen European countries attended the first Geneva Conference on October 26, 1863. Over four days, the delegates drafted a series of resolutions outlining the steps necessary to establish relief societies in their countries. Württemberg, a tiny kingdom in what is now Germany, led the way by setting up the first relief society. By 1875, almost every nation in Europe had its own society to help wounded soldiers in time of war. The volunteer corps became known as Red Cross Societies, which joined under one international federation called the League of Red Cross Societies, founded in 1919.

In 1864, the Committee of Five asked the Swiss government to call a second conference, this time with the aim of developing an international treaty guaranteeing aid for the wounded and protection for relief workers. Delegates from fifteen European nations attended the convention, which opened August 8, 1864, in Geneva. The United States, embroiled in its Civil War at the time, sent a representative but did not participate officially in the discussions.

It took the delegates two weeks to draw up a treaty. The pact's ten articles stipulated that wounded and sick soldiers be treated humanely; established safeguards for relief workers, chaplains, volunteers, and others caring for the wounded; and provided for distinctive flags and armbands, with a red cross on a white background, to be used to identify relief workers, ambulances, and hospitals. The emblem was chosen in honor of Dunant and his homeland of Switzerland, whose national emblem is a white cross on a red background.

Delegates from Baden (now a region in southwestern Germany), Belgium, Denmark, France, Hesse (now a state in central western Germany), Italy, Netherlands, Portugal, Prussia (a former German state now divided among Germany, Russia, and Poland), Spain, Switzerland, and Württemberg signed the Geneva Convention on August 22, 1864. The formal title of the treaty was the 1864 Convention for the Amelioration of the Condition of the Wounded in Armies in the Field. Great Britain, at the time one of the world's most powerful nations, was not an original signer but ratified the treaty on February 18, 1865. For the first time in history a group of nations had agreed to limit their power over enemy soldiers. It was a triumph for the rights of individual human beings.

France became the first nation to ratify the treaty on September 22, 1864. The convention went into effect on June 22, 1865. The International Committee of the Red Cross (ICRC), formerly the Committee of Five, took on the job of overseeing whether nations observed the

The delegates discuss the details of the Geneva Convention of 1864. It was the first international agreement to limit nations' power over enemy soldiers.

treaty's terms, publicizing violations, and intervening on behalf of war victims.

The United States initially refused to sign the treaty. President Abraham Lincoln called it "a fifth wheel on the military coach,"[9] and other American political leaders feared it would entangle the young country in alliances with warring European nations. Although leery of signing the convention, Lincoln supported the precepts on which it was based. During the Civil War, he issued "instructions for the Government of armies of the United States in the Field." The instructions noted that "men who take up arms against one another in public war do not cease on this account to be moral beings, responsible to one another and to God."[10] They stipulated that unarmed citizens should not be attacked, robbed, or harmed; that prisoners of war should be "treated with humanity"; and that yellow flags should be flown over field hospitals so that "the enemy may avoid firing on them."[11]

Despite the similarities between Lincoln's orders and the Geneva Convention, almost two decades would pass before the United States would ratify the international treaty.

Meanwhile, the European nations adhering to the treaty soon put it to use. The red cross emblem received its first test on the battlefield during the war between Prussia and Denmark in 1864. Louis Appia, a Swiss doctor who served on the Committee of Five with Dunant, wore an armband with the red cross while caring for soldiers wounded during the war. Soldiers on both sides recognized the symbol of the red cross and held their fire.

During the Franco-Prussian War of 1870–71, Red Cross workers distributed medical supplies and food to the wounded. Many soldiers had never heard of the treaty, however, and that caused problems for relief workers, who often found themselves in danger. The International Relief Committee for Prisoners of War, under the umbrella of the International Committee of the Red

Cross, set up an information bureau during the same war and appointed a "person of trust" to distribute relief supplies at each prisoner of war camp. The information bureau reported on prisoners, wounded soldiers, and those killed in battle.

The Geneva Convention had stipulated that delegates invite other nations to participate in the treaty. It was the first international treaty to allow additional members to become parties to the convention after it had been signed and ratified. By 1870, all the major nations of Europe and most of the smaller nation-states had agreed to the provisions in the Geneva Convention. Only the United States was missing from the list of major powers to have ratified the convention.

An American nurse, known as the "angel of the battlefield" because of her work in caring for wounded Civil War soldiers, led the effort to win U.S. ratification of the treaty. Clara Barton had gone to Geneva to rest after her Civil War labors. There, she met with Red Cross leaders and became intrigued with the idea of relief societies to care for the wounded. When the war between France and Prussia broke out in 1870, Barton served on the battlefield along with other volunteers.

When she returned home, Barton pushed to get the Geneva Convention ratified by the United States. She had an ally in President James Garfield, who had witnessed her work on Civil War battlefields. Barton formed the first American Red Cross society [the National Society of the Red Cross] in Dansville, New York, in 1881. Shortly after the society's birth, a forest fire devastated the area. Barton and her Red Cross volunteers helped victims of the disas-

Clara Barton and the Red Cross Association in the United States assisted those left homeless by the Johnstown Flood in 1889. Here, volunteers wait outside the Red Cross warehouse, the first building erected in Johnstown after the flood.

ter. It was the first time a Red Cross society had aided people during peacetime.

In September 1881, President Garfield died from wounds suffered when an assassin attacked him in July. Without Garfield's support, Barton feared the Senate wouldn't ratify the Geneva Convention. His successor, Chester Arthur, however, had been impressed with the Red Cross volunteers' work during the forest fire. He agreed to back the ratification effort. In March 1882, the U.S. Senate ratified the Geneva Convention "with complete and astounding unanimity."[12] The nation became the thirty-second country to ratify the pact.

At the time, the action received little notice in the United States. The Senate vote merited only four lines in a Washington, D.C., newspaper. In Europe, however, people were ecstatic that the United States had finally joined other nations supporting the Geneva Convention. Europeans lit bonfires to celebrate when they heard the news of the ratification.[13]

GENEVA CONVENTION OF 1906

The 1885 war between Serbia and Bulgaria was the first in which both sides abided by the Geneva Convention. Relief workers' ability to treat wounded soldiers quickly reduced the death rate to 2 percent, a sure sign that the treaty worked.[14]

The International Committee of the Red Cross met every year to review how well the Geneva Convention was working and to determine whether new provisions were required. It was soon apparent that the treaty needed to be revised. Only a year after the Geneva Convention went into effect, a battle between Austrian and Italian ships illustrated the need for new provisions governing the treatment of the enemy during maritime warfare. On July 20, 1866, during the Battle of Lissa, a fleet of Austrian battleships had rammed and sunk an Italian ship off the Dalmatian coast. The victors ignored the pleas of the helpless Italian sailors; all one hundred of them died in the waters of the Adriatic Sea.

The Swiss government called a second conference at Geneva in October 1868. Representatives of the nations attending the conference adopted fifteen new clauses to the Geneva Convention that would serve to protect combatants at sea as well as to clarify some of the original provisions. Perhaps it was too soon to expect nations to approve more treaty terms. Whatever the reason, the additions to the treaty were never ratified.

Although Red Cross committee members gave up their attempts to revise the treaty that year, the proposed provisions, nevertheless, guided the behavior of armies during two wars. Forces in the Franco-Prussian War of 1870–71 and in the Spanish-American War of 1898 agreed to abide by the Geneva proposals outlining treatment of sailors.

Meanwhile, Russia was taking a lead in efforts to further human rights. Under the leadership of Czar Alexander II, who had freed the serfs in his country in 1861, Russians issued the St. Petersburg Declaration of 1868. The document banned weapons that would cause unnecessary suffering and stipulated that wounded or sick soldiers should not be attacked further. It also defined combatants and civilians, whom, the proclamation noted, should not be harmed if possible.

Alexander had witnessed the toll wars had taken on his country, in both lives and money. He pushed now to limit the devastation caused by war. During the last half of the nineteenth century, the people of Europe had begun to write codes of laws governing everyday life in their countries. With the urging of the czar, they decided to draw up a similar code to apply to behavior in war. To accomplish this, the czar convened the Brussels Conference of 1874. Delegates from fifteen European nations met in July 1874 to review an international pact drawn up by the czar that outlined the rules of warfare. Among other things, the proposed agreement required warring nations to treat prisoners of war (POWs) humanely, banned them from forcing POWs to participate in war efforts, and forced them to pay POWs for any work they were required to do. It was the first international agreement that dealt with the treatment of POWs.

The declaration also adopted the Geneva Convention provisions for sick and wounded soldiers as well as prohibited armies from unnecessarily attacking civilians. One article stipulated: "Family honour and rights, and the lives and property of persons, as well as their religious convictions and their practice, must be respected. Private property cannot be confiscated."[15]

Although the European community supported the International Declaration Concerning the Laws and Customs of War developed at the Brussels Conference and all fifteen of the participants signed it, the nations' governments declined to ratify the document.

Despite the setbacks, proponents of human rights continued to push for some type of international document that would protect both POWs and wounded sailors. After the Brussels Conference, the Institute of International Law, meeting in Geneva, agreed to study that declaration and add its own proposals. The institute, a gathering of world leaders, had formed in 1873 with the goal of developing codes of law that would be accepted by nations throughout the world. The institute's work led to the development of the *Oxford Manual*, a compilation of laws governing warfare. It was adopted September 9, 1880, in Oxford, England. The authors of the codebook had backed away from preparing an international treaty because they believed nations would never ratify it. Instead, they developed guidelines that individual countries could use when writing their own laws on warfare. Among the manual's suggested codes were rules regarding the humane treatment of POWs, respect for civilians, and protection of sick and wounded combatants (again, based on the Geneva Convention).

Czar Nicholas II, grandson of Alexander II, continued his predecessor's attempts to forge a worldwide treaty on the rules of war, including the humane treatment of its victims. In May 1899, he convened a peace conference in the Royal House in the Wood at The Hague, the capital of the Netherlands. The Czar's goal was to pursue "the most effective means of ensuring to all peoples the benefits of a real and lasting peace."[16]

Representatives from twenty-six nations, meeting from May 18 to July 29, 1899, adopted three treaties at the conference. Based on the St. Petersburg Declaration, the

Czar Nicholas II of Russia convened a peace conference at The Hague in 1899, where delegates from twenty-six nations established rules of warfare on land and sea.

Brussels Declaration, and the *Oxford Manual,* the treaties set up rules of war on land and sea and established The Hague Tribunal, a court where nations could settle disputes peacefully instead of going to war.

The members of the International Committee of the Red Cross kept close tabs on the advances made in Brussels and The Hague. While the focus on those meetings was on establishing rules of warfare, the Red Cross committee's primary concern was the treatment of the victims of war. They wanted to make certain that people involved in war at sea would be granted the same protections as soldiers fighting on land. They also wanted to lay down rules requiring that POWs be treated humanely. Although The Hague Conference referred to maritime war, the ICRC believed a more detailed treaty on the subject was needed.

In 1906, the Swiss government, at the request of the International Committee of the Red Cross, called another international conference in Geneva. It was time, members believed, to revise the outdated Geneva Convention of 1864. Delegates from thirty-five nations attended the Geneva sessions, held from June 11 to July 5. The meetings were conducted in French, as they had been at the first Geneva Conference.

The new treaty proposed by the ICRC was much more detailed than the old one. It contained thirty-three articles and eight chapters. The revised convention included new provisions governing the burial of the dead and treatment of combatants at sea, and it required that nations release information on POWs and those wounded or killed in battle.

During the wars that followed the Convention of 1864, the ICRC had discovered some of the treaty provisions didn't work well. The members recommended limiting the role of well-intentioned volunteers who cared for wounded soldiers. Under the new provisions, the civilian volunteers would serve under the supervision of the military but would still be granted "special protection and certain immunities."[17] They also gave official recognition to the Red Cross societies now organized in most nations.

Under the new treaty, warring nations were allowed to send wounded enemy soldiers who were well enough to travel to neutral nations, where they could be interred until the war ended. The first convention had stipulated that recovered soldiers be returned to their homelands "on condition that they shall not again, for the duration of hostilities, take up arms."[18]

All thirty-five nations signed the treaty on July 6, 1906. This time the United States was among them. The U.S. Senate ratified the convention on February 9, 1907, one of the first nations to do so. The Geneva Convention of 1906 became effective August 9, 1907. It replaced the Convention of 1864 for all the nations that had signed both treaties. Nations and nation-states that had signed the earlier convention but did not sign the Convention of 1906—the Holy See, Honduras, and Korea—remained bound by the terms of the 1864 pact. Baden, Bavaria, Congo, Hesse, Mecklenburg-Schwerin, Prussia, Saxony, South African Republic, and Württemberg had signed the 1864 treaty but later became part of other nations and, therefore, were not party to the second Geneva Convention. The Dominican Republic, which ratified the

Signers of Geneva Convention 1906

NORTH AMERICA

United States

CENTRAL AMERICA

Guatemala
Honduras
Mexico
Nicaragua

SOUTH AMERICA

Argentina
Brazil
Chile
Peru
Uruguay

EUROPE

Austria-Hungary
Belgium
Bulgaria
Denmark
France
Germany
Great Britain & Ireland
Greece
Italy
Luxembourg
Montenegro
The Netherlands
Norway
Portugal
Romania
Russia
Serbia
Spain
Sweden
Switzerland

ASIA

China
Japan & Korea
Persia
Siam

AFRICA

Congo

Thirty-five nations from around the world signed the Geneva Convention of 1906. They were Argentina, Austria-Hungary, Belgium, Brazil, Bulgaria, Chile, China, Congo, Denmark, France, Germany, Great Britain and Ireland (one country), Greece, Guatemala, Honduras, Italy, Japan and Korea (one country), Luxemburg, Mexico, Montenegro, the Netherlands, Nicaragua, Norway, Persia, Peru, Portugal, Romania, Russia, Serbia, Siam, Spain, Sweden, Switzerland, the United States, and Uruguay.

treaty on August 25, 1926, was the last nation to accept its terms.

Egypt and Turkey both agreed to the treaty but reserved the right to use a red crescent on a white background instead of a red cross to indicate medical personnel. Iran later used a red lion and sun on its insignia for medical staff, and Israel used a red Star of David. Non-Christian nations objected to use of the red cross because they interpreted it as a symbol of Christianity.

Conference members recommended that nations with questions or disagreements over the terms of the treaty allow The Hague Tribunal to interpret the pact for them. Only Great Britain, Japan, and Korea rejected that proposal. A year later, delegates at the second Hague Peace Conference adopted substantial sections of the Geneva Convention's protections of sailors and POWs as part of its 1907 conventions.

U.S. soldiers fight in the trenches in the Marne River area of France during World War I.

Two

WORLD WAR I

Henri Dunant was right when he predicted that "unhappily we cannot always avoid wars."[1] During the early years of the twentieth century, sporadic fighting broke out between the many nationalistic groups crowded along the Adriatic and Mediterranean Seas. The powerful nations of the region longed to control the region and extend their borders. Germany wanted to reinforce its hold on Alsace-Lorraine, two provinces along the German-French border; Russia hoped to rule Constantinople and the passage between the Black Sea and the Aegean Sea. Austria-Hungary had already overpowered the Serbian province of Bosnia and absorbed that territory into its borders.

The situation was tense when, on June 28, 1914, a Serbian terrorist, Gavrilo Princip, assassinated Archduke Franz Ferdinand of Austria-Hungary at Sarajevo. Austria-Hungary used the incident to declare war on Serbia. Germany, eying a chance to expand its power in the region, backed Austria-Hungary and joined in the declaration of war against Serbia on July 28. The following day, Russian troops amassed along the Austrian border to protect Serbia and its own influence in the region. By the end of August, France, Great Britain, and Japan had entered the fray on the side of the Russians and the Serbs (the Allied Powers). Italy and the United States later joined the Allies and became major combatants in the war. Turkey and Bulgaria joined Germany and Austria-Hungary (the Central Powers). Eventually, the war would rage across the world, involving twenty-eight nations and costing millions of lives.

Reports of the battles, fought in the trenches of Europe, were as grim as those of Henri Dunant. Philip Gibbs, a British war correspondent, described the plight of British soldiers fighting in 1915 in the trenches near Ypres, in northwest Belgium. Covered in mud and lice, the soldiers had to dig through piles of dead bodies to protect themselves from the bombs and mortar fire of the Germans. "Scraps of flesh, booted legs, blackened hands, eyeless heads, came falling over them" whenever the enemy soldiers blew up a mineshaft nearby or aimed bombs at the area.[2]

The death count from these battles was staggering. The British lost almost 250,000 men at Ypres; 500,000 soldiers died in the five-month struggle along the banks of the Somme River in northern France. Soldiers had to face bombs, barbed wire, machine guns from land and the air, and poison gas.

German soldiers fighting along the Somme River were cut off from their supply lines, without food or wa-

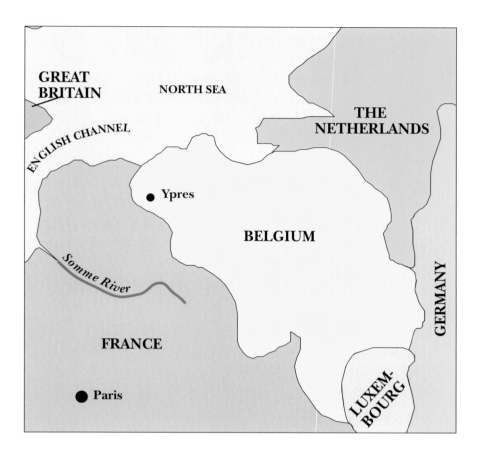

Some of the fiercest fighting during World War I occurred in Ypres, Belgium, and northern France, along the Somme River.

ter. "You can no longer call it war," one German soldier wrote to his wife. "It is mere murder."[3]

On May 7, 1915, a German submarine sank the passenger liner *Lusitania* off the coast of Ireland in the Irish Sea. Almost twelve hundred drowned in the attack, including 124 Americans who had boarded the cruise liner in New York. The Germans used submarines to blockade the waters around Great Britain, France, and Italy and attacked all vessels that entered the area, a violation of international law. The attack on the cruise liner and the sinking of American merchant ships, among other things, led the United States to enter the war on April 2, 1917.

With the support of the Americans, the Allies drove back the German forces. Defeats in Belgium and Italy further damaged the Central Powers. On November 3, 1918, Austria-Hungary agreed to a truce that forced the country to give up its troops and a large strip of its lands. The following week, on November 11, 1918, German leaders signed an armistice.

Almost ten million combatants lost their lives in World War I. Another six million were listed as prisoners and missing, and twenty-one million were wounded. The war had cost the nations involved $200 billion in war supplies and expenses. In addition, towns and cities had been leveled, civilians had been killed and maimed, and personal property had been destroyed.

Until World War I, many people believed war was a legitimate method for nations to resolve disputes, although only as a last resort. The devastation caused by World War I, the War to End All Wars as it was called, left people questioning whether war was ever justified. War itself— with its devastatingly effective modern weapons—had become the ultimate abuser of human rights: It had deprived millions of their right to life.

Wrote newsman Gibbs: "Many men who came out of that conflict were changed, and vowed not to tolerate a system of thought which had led to such a monstrous massacre of human beings who had prayed to the same

God, loved the same joys of life, and had no hatred for one another except as it had been lighted and inflamed by their governors, their philosophers, and their newspapers."[4]

World War I did little to resolve the disputes among the nations involved. The armistice had stopped the fighting, but nothing had been settled. The rivalry between the nations of Europe remained. Even Germany, in its defeat, continued to harbor visions of someday regaining control over its neighbors. Each nation had suffered extraordinary losses with few gains.

U.S. President Woodrow Wilson took the lead in fashioning a peace treaty designed not only to end the war but also to prevent future wars. Primary among the terms was the formation of a League of Nations, a worldwide organization that would settle disputes among nations and oversee terms of the peace treaty.

People throughout the world saw a League of Nations as a great advance for human rights as well as for peace. "The world is hungry for a League of Nations," Florence Harriman, chair of the Commission on Industrial Relations and a Wilson supporter, wrote in March 1919. "It must have a League of Nations. . . . A better chance for education, for housing; and for the female child an opportunity such as has never been dreamt of before— equal opportunity with the men. Surely a new spirit of God is moving in the trees."[5]

To gain European support for the League of Nations, Wilson combined the agreement outlining the terms of peace with Germany and the covenant that set up the league into one treaty, the Treaty of Versailles. The covenant establishing the league banned slavery and guaranteed freedom of religion and conscience to citizens of former colonies protected by the league. It also provided that the former colonists would eventually be granted the right to govern themselves. Other articles in the covenant guaranteed adequate wages to workers, equal pay for equal work, and set forty-eight hours as the standard work week. The pact included a pledge to "endeavour to secure and maintain fair and humane conditions of labour for men, women, and children, both in their own countries and in all countries to which their commercial and industrial relations extend."[6]

The final document, however, was far from the instrument of peace that Wilson had envisioned. France, Great Britain, and Italy had united in their desire to seek revenge on Germany and divide the spoils of war among themselves. The result was a treaty that forced the Germans to accept all the blame for the war; give up territory, resources, and citizens; and pay for war damages. Many believed the treaty, instead of ensuring peace, sowed the seeds of hatred that led to World War II.[7]

Faced with starvation and unrest at home, the Germans finally signed the Treaty of Versailles on June 28, 1919. Wilson, in failing health, returned to the United States to obtain Senate approval of the treaty and the covenant establishing the League of Nations that was a part of it. A hostile reception awaited him. Wilson had lost his power base in the United States when the voters elected a Republican Congress during the November elections of 1918. Many of those who had supported the League of Nations now objected to the compromises

Wilson, in a fruitless campaign to win ratification for the Versailles Treaty

made to appease the British, the French, and the Italians. The Senate refused to ratify the treaty; on March 19, 1920, a bill to support the pact failed by seven votes. It wasn't until July 1921 that the Senate finally passed a resolution that the war had officially ended.

Ultimately, the League of Nations failed. Forty-one nations sent delegates to its first meeting in Geneva on November 15, 1920. Without support from the United States, the organization lacked the prestige it might have had. It was unable to stop Japan's invasions of Manchuria and China and Germany's overthrow of its neighbors, acts that led to World War II.

Before its demise, however, the league advanced the cause of human rights on several fronts. League members signed treaties pledging to respect the rights of minorities within their borders. More than one hundred conventions were adopted regulating labor conditions. In 1926, the league adopted the International Slavery Convention, under which nations agreed to end slavery. The league also set up safe havens for refugees. But perhaps the league's most important role in advancing international human rights was as a model for the United Nations, which would later become the leading force in promoting the rights of mankind.

GENEVA CONVENTION OF 1929

During World War I, the International Committee of the Red Cross had worked hard to see that the terms of the Geneva Conventions were enforced. They established a file of seven million cards to record information on combatants who were wounded, missing, or killed. Families often depended on the card file to learn the fate of their loved ones. Red Cross delegates visited prisoners of war, reported on conditions at POW camps, and did what they could to improve the lot of those held there. After the war, the Red Cross helped reunite POWs with their families.

As the guardian of the Geneva Conventions, the committee realized that the world needed more specific terms to ensure human rights in the increasingly complex business of warfare. Prisoners of war were particularly in need of protection. Though provisions on POWs had been included in the Geneva Convention of 1906 and in The Hague Conventions, they were far too general to offer effective protection to the thousands of prisoners detained during World War I.

Recognizing the need for more detailed regulations, France and Germany had in 1917 and 1918 signed temporary pacts called the Berne Treaties, which regulated operations at POW camps. One provision allowed POWs to choose among their members a committee that would oversee the distribution of supplies and relief aid.

In 1921, delegates gathering in Geneva for the tenth International Red Cross Conference unanimously agreed that the conventions needed to include such details as those specified in the Berne Treaties. They asked the committee to prepare a revised treaty that would include a detailed section on the treatment of POWs. The committee complied, and by 1923 a draft was ready for review.

During this time, the League of Nations was struggling to establish itself as an international broker of peace. Not wanting to interfere with the league's work, perhaps even hoping that the Geneva Conventions would no longer be necessary, the Red Cross delayed presenting the proposed revisions until 1929. By then it was obvious that the league had serious problems and that new provisions were needed to protect the rights of POWs in time of war.

From July 1 to July 27, delegates from forty-seven nations met in Geneva at the invitation of the Swiss government. From the Red Cross drafts, they forged a ninety-seven-article treaty that would replace the Geneva Conventions of 1864 and 1906. Eighty of its articles dealt with the treatment of prisoners of war. The treaty adopted and expanded the POW provisions in The Hague Conventions.

In ancient times, soldiers defeated in war became the property of the victors. In later wars, captured soldiers were killed, tortured, or held for ransom. Such behavior, the delegates warned, was no longer tolerable in the world of the twentieth century. It was the duty of every nation, read the preamble to the new Geneva Convention, "to mitigate as far as possible, the inevitable rigors [of war] and to alleviate the condition of prisoners of war."[8]

Much of the convention was based on the principles set forth by Jean Jacques Rousseau regarding war. Rousseau, an eighteenth-century French political philosopher, had written that war was conducted between nations, not individuals. As such, individual soldiers were not natural enemies. As soon as they surrendered (or were captured), they ceased to become enemies, and the opposing side had no right to kill them.[9]

The new provisions required that POWs be humanely

treated. For the first time in a treaty, healthy prisoners were described as victims of war and, as such, were entitled to the protections that covered sick and wounded soldiers in previous conventions. They were entitled to practice their religion, could write wills, and retain their personal belongings (with the exception of military goods).

In another important first, the Convention of 1929 established the role of neutral countries, called Protecting Powers, as protectors of POWs. The neutral mediators could negotiate better treatment for POWs and help resolve disputes over POW treatment between two warring nations. Under the terms of the convention, the mediators were allowed to visit POW camps, talk alone with POWs, and act as referees when POWs had complaints against their captors. Switzerland, traditionally a neutral country, later served as mediator for thirty-five countries at one time, under the terms of the convention. The role of neutral mediators became "one of the indispensable guarantees of the Geneva law."[10]

A third significant provision prohibited captors from punishing POWs for complaining to mediators. They were also barred from punishing POWs as a way to get back at the enemy or to retaliate when the enemy treated their captive soldiers badly.

The treaty established the right of POWs to elect other prisoners to represent them and set forth the duties of the POW representatives. It banned any use of torture or humiliation and set down a strict code that governed the handling of POWs who misbehaved. POWs were entitled to hearings or trials and could not be punished for actions not committed by them personally.

Russian prisoners at work in a German POW camp during World War I

Under the treaty, captors could not use POWs to work in the war effort. If they performed other work, they were entitled to payment and fair treatment. They could be held as prisoners, but not confined in jails or isolation cells. Those who died in captivity were entitled to a proper burial; those who survived would be released to their countries' leaders immediately after the war.

The treaty also gave the Red Cross the job of collecting information on POWs and overseeing conditions where they were held.

The delegates made revisions in other areas of the treaty based on experiences in World War I. Previous conventions stipulated that the treaty terms applied only if all nations involved in a war had agreed to the convention. During World War I, Montenegro (a tiny republic along the Adriatic Sea) had not signed The Hague Convention. It was argued that all the warring nations, therefore, could ignore the terms of the convention. The nations agreed to abide by the treaty anyway, but there was no guarantee they would do the same under similar circumstances in future wars.

To correct this oversight, the Geneva delegates required nations that ratified the new treaty to abide by its terms whenever they dealt with other nations that had ratified it. If nations that had not approved the treaty were also involved, temporary pacts could be made with them. Their presence, however, would not cancel out the duties of treaty nations to one another.

The new treaty also extended protection to planes used to transport medical supplies and the wounded. A red cross (or crescent or lion and sun), painted on the plane, would identify it as a medical carrier.

The representatives of all forty-seven nations attending the conference signed the treaty on July 27, 1929. It became effective June 19, 1931. Before the delegates ended their work, they recommended another conference be held soon to draw up provisions to protect civilians in war. They were particularly concerned about the treatment of foreigners whose adopted homelands became embroiled in wars with their native countries. Little had been written to ensure their protection or the safety of civilians whose homeland was occupied by enemy armies.

Following the delegates' advice, the International Committee of the Red Cross began preparing a treaty designed to protect the human rights of civilians during war. At a meeting of the ICRC in Tokyo in 1934, representatives from around the world approved a preliminary draft of the new treaty. The nations of the world received drafts of a new Geneva Convention, including the separate treaty on the protection of civilians, in January 1939. They were asked to review the provisions to prepare for a world conference to be held in Geneva in early 1940, when the treaties would be considered.

The new convention consisted of four separate treaties. The first and second dealt with wounded and sick combatants on land and sea. The third expanded the protections of prisoners of war and regulated their treatment in even more detail than in the Convention of 1929. It was the fourth treaty, however, that gained the most attention. For the first time, the delegates would consider a comprehensive code of behavior governing warring nations in their dealings with civilians. Surely, these innocent victims of war deserved the protections of the Geneva Conventions.

The Conference of 1940 was never held. Before the Swiss government could convene the meeting, another world war erupted, unparalleled in its vicious slaughter of men, women, and children. In its wake, mankind saw the disastrous consequences of its failure to bind the nations of the world to a treaty guaranteeing basic human rights to civilians caught in the horror of war.[11]

Hitler and his Nazi staff touring Nuremberg

THREE

WORLD WAR II

Germany, under dictator Adolf Hitler and his Nazi followers, invaded Poland on September 1, 1939. England and France immediately demanded that the German leader withdraw his troops. When Hitler refused, the two countries declared war on Germany on September 3, 1939.

Thus began a war marked by human rights abuses so massive that it was almost incomprehensible. Fortified with a powerful array of modern weaponry, from submarines to armored tanks to dive bombers, the Germans quickly mowed down Polish resistance and marched on to capture Denmark and Norway.

By the end of May 1940, Belgium, the Netherlands, and Luxembourg had fallen to German forces. Advancing German tanks broke through the French line, and on June 24, that country signed an armistice with Hitler. Nazi sympathizers within the French government allied with Germany. French resisters, led by General Charles de Gaulle, joined British forces in their fight against the Germans.

With the fall of France, Hitler trained his guns on Great Britain. Beginning in August, German bombers blasted England in almost daily air raids that targeted seaports and industrial centers throughout the island nation. The Royal Air Force, with only a few hundred planes, managed to hold off an invasion in what became known as the Battle of Britain. By the end of the year, the saucy British spitfires had shot down 2,500 Nazi planes.

On September 7, 1940, the Nazi's Luftwaffe bombers shifted tactics and began all-out night attacks on London. The German planes, more than six hundred strong, dove low over London, dropping their deadly cargo on the citizens below. In minutes more than four hundred people lost their lives and fourteen hundred more suffered injuries from the attack. As the city burned, people struggled from the rubble to help firefighters quell the fires. "The London that we knew was burning," wrote one eyewitness—"the London which had taken thirty generations of men a thousand years to build . . . and the Nazis had done that in thirty seconds."[1]

For the next fifty-seven nights, the German planes rained bombs on the English capital. But the haughty Nazi minister of aviation, Hermann Göring, who had boasted that the Luftwaffe fleet would knock the Royal Air Force out of the skies, encountered more than he bargained for in the determined British. Amid the piles of demolished buildings, broken windows, and splintered walls, paper British flags flew in the breeze. Merchants served their customers in shops without windows or

More than four hundred people lost their lives and another fourteen hundred were injured in an attack by German bombers on London on September 7, 1940.

doors. Sleeping in bomb shelters and basements, Londoners managed to joke, share anecdotes, and carry on despite their city falling down around them.[2] Children were sent to the countryside for safety.

Italy had joined the war on the side of Germany in June 1940. In September Japan took advantage of the war to seek control of China and the rest of Asia. On September 27, Japan, Germany, and Italy signed a pact that united the three nations as the Axis powers. The agreement put Japan in charge of eastern Asia, while Italy and Germany shared control of Europe.

Great Britain fought on, defending its Mediterranean strongholds in Gibraltar and the Suez Canal. Germany managed to seize control of the Balkan nations of Romania, Hungary, Bulgaria, Yugoslavia, and Greece. Meanwhile, the United States, although not directly involved in the war, supplied the British with vital warplanes, artillery, tanks, and other war supplies.

Russia and Germany had signed a pact in 1939 in which the two nations agreed not to interfere with each other. During June of 1941, however, Russia suddenly became the focus of the Nazi war effort. On June 22, 1941, Germany attacked the Russian army along its two thousand-mile eastern border. As the Russian army retreated, it burned fields, crops, manufacturing plants—anything that might benefit the Nazi troops.

Meanwhile, Japanese forces began their push to take over the lands in southeastern Asia and China. The Japanese government ignored the demands of England and the United States to stop its aggressive acts. Instead, the Japanese said they wanted peace and sent an official

*On Sunday, December 7, 1941, 189 Japanese bombers struck
the American fleet stationed in Pearl Harbor, Hawaii, sinking
the U.S.S.* Arizona *and several other battleships and killing
3,500 people.*

to Washington, D.C., to talk with U.S. President Franklin
D. Roosevelt. It was a delaying tactic.

On Sunday, December 7, 1941, at 7:30 A.M., 189
Japanese bombers struck the American fleet stationed in
Pearl Harbor, Hawaii. The bombs damaged all eight of

61

the U.S. battleships at the dock and killed 3,500 people, many of them civilians. The following day, Congress overwhelmingly approved a declaration of war against Japan. On December 11, Germany and Italy joined Japan in declaring war against the United States. Several South American nations soon joined the war on the side of the Allies. By the end of 1941, twenty-six nations had lined up against the Axis Powers.

In early 1942, the war heated up in the Pacific. After fierce battles at Bataan and Corregidor, the Japanese seized control of the Philippines. More than thirty-six thousand American and Filipino soldiers surrendered to the Japanese forces in April. On May 6, the Japanese captured another eleven thousand men who had escaped to the island of Corregidor. Rounded up by the Japanese, the American and Filipino soldiers—hands tied behind their backs—were forced on a brutal march from Bataan to prison camps in the northern part of the Philippines. Most of the men marched fifty-five miles from Bataan north to San Fernando and taken further north by rail to the town of Capas. The weary prisoners were then forced to march an additional eight miles to Camp O'Donnell, which the Japanese used as a POW camp. This forced evacuation became known as the Bataan Death March. More than seventeen thousand prisoners died during the march through the steamy jungles of the Philippines.

While the Japanese flexed their muscles in the Pacific, the German forces began to lose ground. In October, the British, after initial losses, stopped the Nazis at El Alamein in Egypt along the Mediterranean Sea. By early November, the British, under the command of General

Bernard L. Montgomery, had managed to force the Germans out of Egypt. American troops led by General Dwight D. Eisenhower were having similar successes in French North Africa. In November, they gained control of Algeria and Morocco.

At the same time, determined Russian forces fought off German soldiers in Stalingrad, the beginning of a long battle that eventually forced the Nazis to retreat to Poland.

By 1943, British and American bombers—taking their lead from the Luftwaffe raids earlier in the war—were bombarding German cities day and night. The bombing, which was to continue until the end of the war, turned major cities into piles of rubble. Railroads and bridges were blown apart, and industrial centers were reduced to twisted chunks of steel and splintered glass. Homes, churches, hospitals, and office buildings lay in ruins, as they did in London after the German attacks.

As horrendous as the bombings were, the Jews in Europe faced an even greater horror: the extermination of their people. At the end of World War I, many Germans believed they could have won the war if their efforts had not been undercut by the Communists and Socialists, who were accused of placing their loyalty to a global movement above love of their country. Many of the movement's leaders were Jewish, and Adolf Hitler used the German bitterness toward the Socialists to focus hatred on the Jews.[3] Beginning in 1933, Hitler began rounding up Jews, Gypsies, Slavs, and others, and detaining them in concentration camps. That same year, the nation withdrew from the League of Nations.

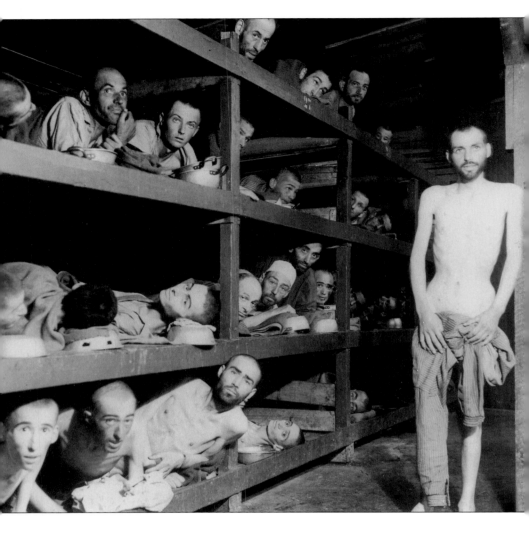

*Captives held in the Nazi concentration camp at Buchenwald.
Many of those held there died before U.S. troops arrived to free
them.*

The German government, under Hitler's leadership, passed a series of laws, known as the Nuremberg Laws, that denied Jews basic rights, forced them to give up their property, and expelled their children from school. By 1941, Germany had undertaken a massive deportation of Jews to concentration camps in Buchenwald in eastern Germany and Dachau, near Munich. The Nazis soon sent Jews in Poland, Austria, Hungary, Russia, the Netherlands, and other areas under German control to the camps as well or herded them into ghettos. After a rebellion among Polish Jews, the Nazis sent three hundred thousand from the Warsaw Ghetto to the Treblinka death camp in Poland. Another uprising in 1943 led to the extermination of the people in the Warsaw Ghetto in May 1943.

Once at the camps, thousands of Jews were lined up and marched into crematoriums, where they were gassed to death. Nazi doctors used others, including many children, as guinea pigs for painful and often fatal medical experiments. Many died of starvation in the camps. Altogether, six million Jews and nine million other civilians died at the hands of the Nazis. The extermination of people because of their race, religion, or nationality is called genocide. The Holocaust—the Nazi massacres—was the worst genocide the world had ever seen.

The death toll continued to climb in 1944 as the warring nations engaged in one fierce battle after another. The Russians continued to push the German army back toward its own borders. Allied forces overtook Rome in June 1944. On June 6, D day, American and British troops landed on the beaches of Normandy, on the northwestern region of France along the English Channel. With losses of about 40,000, the Allied forces battled their way inland until, on August 25, they seized control of Paris. By September, the Allies had crossed into Germany, defeating the Nazi troops defending Aachen, a city along the Belgian border.

Fiercely defending their territory, the Germans attacked the Allied lines on December 16, 1944, in the Ardennes, a plateau that runs along northern France, Belgium, and Luxembourg. Nazis, a few of whom were wearing stolen American uniforms and driving American trucks, forced a "bulge" in the lines of the surprised Allied troops that extended sixty miles wide and forty-five miles deep. The Battle of the Bulge, as the offensive came to be known, took the lives of 220,000 German soldiers and forty thousand Allied forces. The American troops regained their foothold, and by the end of March the Allies had penetrated deep into Germany.

Squeezed between the advancing Russian troops and Allied soldiers driving across the Rhine, the Germans made a futile last stand in Berlin in April 1945. To avoid capture, Hitler committed suicide on April 30 as the Russians took control of the burning German capital. The Germans surrendered May 7, 1945.

Meanwhile, U.S. General Douglas MacArthur's forces had retaken the Philippines in July 1945. Although the Allies effectively controlled much of the Pacific islands, Japanese soldiers continued to fight. Kamikaze pilots flew suicide missions, diving their fighter planes into American ships at Okinawa.

On August 6, the *Enola Gay* circled the skies above the

The Japanese city of Hiroshima lay in ruins from an atomic bomb dropped by the United States on August 6, 1945.

Japanese city of Hiroshima. At 8:15 A.M., with no sign of enemy planes, the U.S. bomber dropped an atomic bomb with the force of about twenty thousand tons of TNT on the city. The bomb leveled a five-square-mile area, destroying three-fifths of Hiroshima. When Japan refused to surrender, President Harry S Truman, who had taken over the post at the death of Franklin D. Roosevelt on

April 12, 1945, ordered a second bomb dropped on Nagasaki. That bomb, detonated August 9, destroyed about 1.8 square miles in the heart of the city. It was estimated that up to 140,000 people died in the two bombings. Many thousands more died as the result of burns or radiation-induced disease caused by the nuclear explosion. Japan officially surrendered on September 2, 1945, aboard the U.S.S. *Missouri.* The war was finally over.

The toll of dead and wounded from World War II was too high to count. Many bodies lay buried forever under bomb-wrecked buildings. No one knew how many were killed in China and other Asian territories. Historians now believe that at least fifty million people lost their lives in the war.[4]

The human rights abuses during the war had been monumental. Millions of civilians had been killed, massacred in German concentration camps, blown to bits by air attacks in England and Germany, burned to death by radiation fallout from the world's most powerful bombs in Japan.

If World War I had not convinced the people of the world that war was not an acceptable means to settle disputes, the horrors of World War II certainly reinforced the message. People everywhere supported the establishment of a strong world body—much like that attempted by the League of Nations—that would help ensure peace and protect human rights.

President Roosevelt and British Prime Minister Winston Churchill made the initial steps toward such a goal during secret meetings in the North Atlantic August 9–12, 1941. The Atlantic Charter, arising from that con-

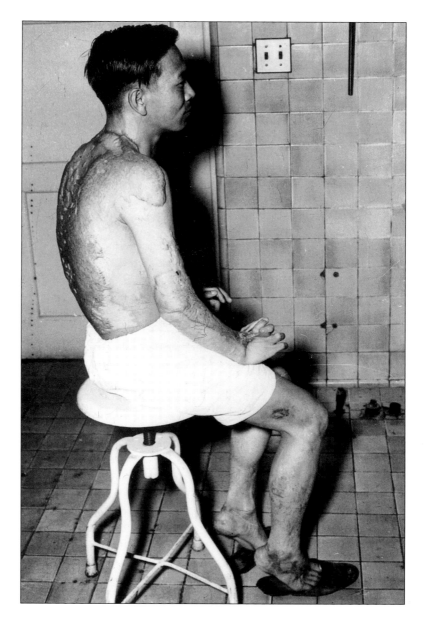

A victim of the bomb blast in Hiroshima

ference aboard the U.S.S. *Augusta*, declared the two nations' commitment to worldwide peace and to peaceful settlement of disputes after the war.

Representatives from the United States, Great Britain, Russia, and China met at Dumbarton Oaks in Washington, D.C., in September 1944 and drew up plans for an association of world powers—the United Nations, which would help ensure peace after the war had ended. Meeting with Churchill and Russian leader Joseph Stalin in Yalta in February 1945, Roosevelt pushed the plan further by winning Soviet support for a General Assembly made up of delegates from all member nations and a Security Council, which gave vetoes to the major powers.

Even before the official end of the war, delegates from fifty nations gathered in San Francisco on April 25, 1945, to formulate a charter and to open the first meeting of the United Nations. Roosevelt was scheduled to open the conference, but thirteen days before the meeting, he suffered a cerebral hemorrhage and died. The U.S. delegation, with the support of President Truman, took their seats at the UN Assembly without the leader who had done so much to ensure its organization. "One feels in the San Francisco Conference that a strong hand is missing," wrote Eleanor Roosevelt of her late husband. "I am sad that he could not see the end of his long work which he carried so magnificently."[5]

Based on the Atlantic Charter, the UN charter adopted at San Francisco made it clear that human rights was an international matter. It stated as one of its goals a determination "to reaffirm faith in fundamental human rights" and gave individuals somewhere to turn if their country's government did not protect their rights or if, indeed, their homeland violated their rights.[6] On June 26, the delegates signed the charter establishing the United Nations.

In Washington, Eleanor Roosevelt, so recently First Lady and now private citizen, urged the Senate to support the United Nations. She viewed the organization as her husband's legacy and stressed the importance of passing the charter immediately.[7] The members of the Senate, with the horror of the atomic bomb's destruction fresh in their minds, ratified the charter by a vote of 89 to 2 on July 28. Two Republican senators, William Langer of North Dakota and Henrik Shipstead of Minnesota, cast the opposing votes. By October 24, enough nations had ratified the charter to make the United Nations an official organization. This time the United States would give its full backing to the world body.

Former First Lady Eleanor Roosevelt played a major role in the passage of the UN's Universal Declaration of Human Rights.

FOUR

UNIVERSAL HUMAN RIGHTS

Eleanor Roosevelt, dressed in black and towering over many of the men in the room, walked determinedly to her seat in Westminster Hall in London. On one side sat the delegate from the Soviet Union; on the other, the other members of the American delegation. At sixty-one, she was about to undertake one of the most important, and strenuous, assignments of her life.

Mrs. Roosevelt, one of the few women delegates attending the first meeting of the United Nations Assembly, was ready for the challenge. Since her husband had died in April 1945, she had been searching for a job that would occupy her considerable energies. The United Nations had always appealed to her; for years she had been a booster of the concept of a peacekeeping world body.

Appointed to the post by President Harry Truman, Mrs. Roosevelt would serve as a member of Committee III, dealing with human rights. For days, crossing the Atlantic aboard the *Queen Elizabeth,* she had prepared for her work as a delegate, reading the briefing papers compiled for her by the State Department and conferring with advisers.

Now, as the first session opened in January 1946, she joined the other delegates in electing a president to lead the UN Assembly in its monumental work. In accepting the post, Paul Henri Spaak, foreign minister of Norway, paid tribute to Eleanor and Franklin Roosevelt for their support of the United Nations. "There is one delegate," he said, "to whom I wish to extend particular sympathy and tribute. . . . I do not think it would be possible to begin at this Assembly without mentioning her and the name of the late President Roosevelt."[1]

The fledgling organization suffered from many of the same problems that had plagued the League of Nations. None of the big nations wanted to hand their power over to a world body. Following the lead of the league, the United Nations had been organized with a Security Council composed of fifteen members that gave veto power to each of the five major powers: the United States, the Soviet Union, China, Great Britain, and France. Several people pushed for a true world government where each nation had an equal voice, but Mrs. Roosevelt understood how impractical such a plan was:

> Russia would be out at once and our Congress would never have let us go in. We couldn't get any one of the big three powers to give up their veto. We will have to crawl together, running will be out of the question until all of us have gained far

more confidence in each other than we now have.[2]

After sitting through long sessions devoted to ironing out the rules of procedure, delegates finally began work in their committees. Almost immediately, tensions boiled over in Committee III. The controversy centered on the opposing views on refugees held by the Western delegates and those representing the Soviet bloc. The Communists put refugees into two categories: those who wanted to return to their countries and those who were traitors. They wanted to put limits on speech and information circulated at refugee camps and to allow the governments of the refugees' native lands to run the camps.

After the committee voted down their proposals, the determined Soviets took the matter before the UN Assembly, where all member nations could consider it. Eleanor Roosevelt squared off against the Soviet delegate, Andrei Vishinsky, over the issue. Vishinsky argued that the refugees—about one million, most of whom had fled Communist regimes—should be returned to their countries. It was not an international affair at all, he argued, but the responsibility of the individual nations.

But Mrs. Roosevelt used the example of Spain in her rebuttal. There, the harsh rule of General Francisco Franco had forced many Spanish nationals to flee their country. Mrs. Roosevelt argued that, under the Soviet plan, these Spanish refugees would be forced to return to "a fascist country," where they would be in danger. She supported people's right to free speech and the right to make decisions for themselves. "Are we so weak in the

UN," she asked, "that we are going to forbid human beings the right to hear what their friends believe? It is their right to say it and their right to hear it and make their own decision."[3]

She implored the delegates to adopt policies "which will consider first the rights of man, which will consider what makes man more free: not governments but man!"[4] The UN Assembly sided with Mrs. Roosevelt "hands down."[5]

Hitler's outrageous disregard for human rights had led the United Nations to include prominently in its charter a guarantee of those rights to all people. Eleanor Roosevelt agreed to chair the small committee that would develop a plan for establishing a Commission on Human Rights. Meeting in the library of Hunter College in New York City, the committee worked for three weeks in April and May 1946. It ended its sessions with a recommendation to the UN Economic and Social Council on the setup of a permanent eighteen-nation Commission on Human Rights. It also proposed that the commission prepare an international bill of rights.

The delegates met in New York when the United Nations Assembly reconvened in October 1946. Mrs. Roosevelt, the U.S. delegate on the new Human Rights Commission, was once again chosen as chair. The commission soon began its work on developing an international bill of rights. John Humphrey, director of the United Nations' Human Rights Division, undertook the difficult job of preparing the first draft. It was a tricky business. The document had to address the demand by Western nations for individual freedoms such as those specified in the U.S.

Bill of Rights, and for economic and social rights such as job security and housing called for by the Soviets and Socialists.

Initially, most members of the commission wanted to draw up a treaty at the same time that would require members to enforce the provisions of the international bill of rights. It soon became clear, however, that neither the Soviet Union nor the United States would readily ratify such a treaty. By this time, both countries were embroiled in a cold war that pitted them against each other on almost every issue. The United States did not want to be committed to a treaty that it believed the Soviets would not live up to. Southern leaders also feared that the treaty might be used to force the country to aid black Americans in their push for civil rights.[6]

To avoid delay, the commission finally decided to consider the bill of rights and the treaty separately to ensure that at least the former would be approved quickly. In June 1947, a subcommittee of delegates met to review Humphrey's draft. It was then sent to the member nations for their review.

Reconvening in Geneva in November, the commission worked long days revising, discussing, and debating the merits of the bill of rights. Mrs. Roosevelt was so determined to finish work on the document that she sometimes kept the members working until seven at night. One weary delegate urged her "not to forget the rights of the human beings who were members of the Commission."[7]

At last, in mid-December, the commission voted 13 to 4 to approve a draft of the Universal Declaration of Human Rights, the official name of the bill of rights document. The commission, however, still had a bit more work to do. At Mrs. Roosevelt's suggestion, the members agreed to simplify the language in the bill so that it would be "readily understood by all peoples."[8]

After consulting with their governments, the commission met again in May to work out a final draft of the declaration. The Russian delegate pushed for the addition of a phrase that would have put the government in charge of making sure rights were granted its citizens. But the commission declined to make the change. When it came time for a vote on the final version of the declaration, the Soviets abstained. The rest of the commission members approved the document on June 18, 1948.

There was still one more hurdle to overcome—the commission had to win the support of Committee III before the declaration could be brought to the UN General Assembly for a vote. When Committee III reviewed the declaration, the Western nations and the Soviet bloc renewed their debate on the issue. A frustrated Mrs. Roosevelt waited while the committee spent eighty-five meetings discussing the declaration before finally sending it to the UN General Assembly for a vote.[9]

After a debate that lasted late into the night, the UN General Assembly voted on December 10, 1948, to approve the declaration. Forty-eight nations supported the measure, eight—including the Soviet bloc—abstained, and two were not present for the vote. The session ended with a standing ovation for Mrs. Roosevelt.

The Universal Declaration reiterated the rights stated in the U.S. Bill of Rights and later Amendments to the

Eleanor Roosevelt, center, listens through earphones to the proceedings of the United Nations General Assembly held in New York City.

U.S. Constitution: the right to life and liberty, the right to be free from slavery and torture, and the right to equal treatment before the law. It gave people the right to leave their countries and return if they wished, and the right to own property. Freedom of religion and expression and the right to choose one's own government were also guaranteed. The declaration also included a list of social and economic rights, advocated by the Socialists: the right to work, to equal pay for equal work, to rest and reasonable working hours, to an adequate standard of living, and to education.

Because it was a declaration and not a treaty, the document did not require ratification by the member nations. Even though the declaration was not binding, its effect on world recognition of human rights was far-reaching. The European Convention on Human Rights and the court that oversees its enforcement are two tangible results of the declaration. It has also been used as the basis of laws in many countries, in other UN resolutions, and by those fighting for human rights throughout the world.

The declaration, wrote Adlai Stevenson in 1961, "has entered the consciousness of the people of the world, has shaped their aspirations, and has influenced the consciences of nations."[10]

GENEVA CONVENTIONS OF 1949

The atrocities of World War II demonstrated to the members of the International Committee of the Red Cross that a new treaty on the treatment of civilians was urgently needed. One hopeful sign to emerge from the war, however, was that prisoners of war had fared better than those in World War I. This improvement was largely due to the 1929 convention on POWs.

According to Red Cross records, POWs held in camps where the Geneva Conventions were observed died at just about the same rate as civilians. In camps where the convention provisions were ignored, however, deaths rose 30 percent to 90 percent above the normal rate. In German camps, where human rights compacts were ignored, three-fifths of the POWs died before the war ended.[11]

During the war, Red Cross representatives made eleven thousand visits to POW camps and shipped two thousand freight cars per month full of relief goods to prisoners, beginning in 1943. Their international card index recorded the status of forty million soldiers.[12]

This evidence that the system worked, at least in part, to ease the suffering of war victims encouraged the committee to continue its efforts. Using its drafts developed in the 1930s, the International Committee of the Red Cross set out to incorporate the lessons learned in World War II. Although the committee strongly supported the work of the United Nations, it was well aware of the need for written rules of humane treatment. The Cold War was increasing tensions between the West and the Soviet bloc, uprisings in Korea and other developing countries were a threat to peace, and people wanted stronger legal guarantees to protect humanity from future atrocities.

The Red Cross committee convened several meetings in Geneva to review the drafts. Government experts met in 1947 to add their suggestions. The drafts were also re-

American Red Cross workers confer with Nazi medical corps-
men outside a French cafe. The cafe was used by the Nazi Red
Cross before the area fell to Allied forces.

viewed by representatives from several nations, Red Cross societies, and other groups.

At the request of the Red Cross, the Swiss government invited the nations of the world to Geneva once again to prepare yet another set of conventions. Fifty-nine nations answered the call, and four others sent representatives to observe the proceedings.

For almost four months, from April 21 to August 12, the delegates to the seventeenth International Red Cross Conference hammered out provisions in four treaties. They dealt with revisions to the conventions governing the treatment of wounded and sick soldiers and of those involved in maritime war, new provisions regulating POWs, and, for the first time, a separate treaty on the treatment of civilians.

The delegates often disagreed on the exact wording of the treaties. But working together, they clung to a common goal: to protect the humanity—the innate rights—of those entangled in war. "The discussions were dominated throughout by a common horror of war and a determination to mitigate the sufferings of war victims," wrote Jean de Preux, a member of the legal department of the ICRC.[13]

It soon became obvious that some parts of the treaties needed special attention. The delegates referred the provisions on which they disagreed to a special committee set up for that purpose in May. The committee held twenty-six meetings during the spring and summer to resolve the differences. Groups of experts also reviewed various segments of the treaties. In all, the committees held eighty-eight meetings, including thirty-six by the main ICRC.[14]

The hard work resulted in four treaties with more than four hundred articles among them. The delegates made it clear that the treaties were for the benefit of individuals, not nations, and that people's right to humane treatment was not something that could be negotiated. For example, even if both battling nations claimed they were not at war, people taken prisoner would still be protected by the Geneva Convention on POWs.

"It must not be forgotten that the Conventions have been drawn up first and foremost to protect individuals, and not to serve State interests," de Preux pointed out in his commentary on the POW treaty.[15] In a later section, he noted: "The requirement that protected persons must at all times be humanely treated is the basic theme of the Geneva Conventions. . . . With regard to the concept of humanity, the purpose of the Convention is none other than to define the correct way to behave towards a human being."[16]

Convention IV, setting forth the rights of civilians who find themselves caught up in war, received the most attention. Designed in good part as a response to the atrocities perpetrated by Hitler's Nazis on the civilian populations of Europe, the convention presented nations with a humanitarian rule book to follow. The treaty allowed nations at war to set up safety zones where the wounded, sick, old, and young could escape from the war. Expectant mothers and mothers of children under the age of seven would also be allowed to stay in the safety zones.

According to the terms of the treaty, the zones could be established during peacetime or after the outbreak of war. If nations were unable to agree on the zones, the Red

Cross or other neutral party could help establish them. Once the zones were set up and identified, the warring nations were banned from attacking them.

Similar provisions allowed the establishment of neutral zones, either in the country at war or in a neutral country, where people not involved in the war effort could go. Wounded and sick people, either civilians or soldiers, could stay in the neutral zone, as could people not working in war-related fields. For example, workers at munitions plants wouldn't qualify to live in a neutral zone, but those teaching school would.

Under the treaty, nations were not allowed to force people to leave their homes unless their lives were in danger. Even in that case, people could be moved only as a temporary measure and must be permitted to return to their homes after the crisis had passed. This provision, written to prevent events such as Hitler's mass deportation of Jews, could also have applied to actions taken by the United States during World War II. In the aftermath of Japan's attack on Pearl Harbor, President Franklin D. Roosevelt had ordered the forced removal of thousands of Japanese American families from West Coast states to detention camps. Despite claims that the move was a "military necessity," no proof was offered that these citizens posed a threat to American security.

The treaty also allowed civilians who lived in a territory that was occupied by the enemy or who were alien residents of a warring nation to move from their homes. If a nation prevented the move, citizens could take their case to court or before a neutral board.

Like POWs and wounded soldiers, civilians should be

treated humanely, the treaty decreed. They were entitled, "in all circumstances, to respect for their persons, their honour, their family rights, their religious convictions and practices, and their manners and customs."[17] The treaty banned murder, torture, abuse, mutilation, and medical or scientific experiments. Enemy nations were banned from intimidating or terrorizing civilians under their control, nor could they legally confiscate personal property or belongings.

Bending to political pressure from various nations, the delegates allowed military leaders to make some exceptions to the treaty rules if an "imperative military necessity" existed (for example, in their decision to move civilians). Another political hot potato involved bombing raids. The treaty offered no protection to civilians from enemy bombing raids, which had claimed the lives of hundreds of thousands in England, Germany, and Japan. Delegates believed that the Allied countries would refuse to sign the treaty if it contained a provision that put their bombing activities in a bad light. Unfortunately, because of this omission, thousands of civilians in Vietnam and Korea found themselves with no legal protection against such raids during the wars that later devastated their homelands.[18]

Despite the treaty's imperfections, delegates clung to their overall goal of protecting human rights. The nations that signed the treaty on civilians pledged to abide by a new humanitarian code that set forth "the high moral standards expected of civilized peoples who tragically find themselves at war."[19] Granted, some nations might fail to live up to the pledge—Hitler had ordered his men to disregard the Geneva and The Hague Conventions before they attacked Russia.[20] But the nations that did keep the code would spare the lives and honor the rights of thousands of people who otherwise would have been killed. For them, the value of the Geneva Conventions was beyond measure.

The third convention adopted by the delegates expanded the provisions of the treaty on POWs. Jean de Preux, in his commentary on the treaty, noted that the right to humane treatment is "valid at all times." Rules of conduct are most needed, de Preux wrote, when people have no other defense—when they are in prison and at the mercy of an enemy. "It is in such situations, when human values appear to be in greatest peril, that the provision assumes its full importance."[21]

The delegates, with the abuses of World War II in mind, included new provisions banning medical experiments and mutilation on POWs. They also established rules for female POWs, protecting them from rape, assault, and forced prostitution and requiring that separate facilities be set up to ensure their privacy.

The treaty added resistance fighters to the list of people considered to be POWs—and thus protected by the convention. It also stipulated that people captured by an enemy should be treated as POWs even if war had not been declared. The treaty's protections also were applied to those captured when an enemy occupies a territory, even if there is no armed resistance. During World War II, several nations had surrendered to Nazi control without a fight.

In its 143 articles, the treaty provided a much more

detailed set of rules to follow regarding POWs. It further defined where and how they could be detained, outlined labor regulations, and described court proceedings to be used against them. As in previous treaties, POWs could not be tortured, murdered, or humiliated. "The aim of the Convention," de Preux noted, "is certainly to grant prisoners of war in enemy hands a protection which will preserve their human dignity and prevent their being brought down to the level of animals."[22]

Previous treaties required that POWs be released at the end of a war. But during World War II, several nations did not agree to an armistice (ceasefire) or officially sign a treaty ending the war. As a result, some POWs remained prisoners for up to four years after the fighting stopped. To remedy that, the delegates at the 1949 conference required that POWs be released immediately after active hostilities ended. The delegates also stipulated that the provisions of the treaty be posted at all POW camps.

Jean de Preux wrote that "of all the statements made on the international level with regard to the individual human being," the POW pact had been the one that had been observed more closely than any other.[23] He noted with optimism that nations' ability to agree on the treatment of POWs was a good sign that they might expand human rights in other circumstances as well. "The fact that men can reach agreement to apply such an advanced and balanced statute to the enemy in war-time," he wrote, "should be seen as a good omen for other endeavours aimed at giving the individual his rightful place in the modern world and thus establishing a better equilibrium."[24]

Conventions I and II updated the provisions in previous Geneva Conventions and The Hague Conventions concerning the sick and wounded in war on land and sea.

Seventeen delegates signed all four conventions on the last day of the conference, August 12, 1949. Others signed at a special meeting in December and in intervals after that date. By February 12, 1950, representatives from sixty-one nations had signed the four treaties.

Switzerland and Yugoslavia became the first to ratify the conventions when their governments voted on the issue April 21, 1950, a little more than a year after the delegates first gathered in Geneva. Six months later, on October 21, 1950, three of the four conventions went into effect in those countries. The maritime convention became effective a year later. By the end of 1958, seventy-four nations had ratified the four treaties, including the United States and the Soviet Union.

Today, almost all the nations of the world have ratified or accepted the terms of the Geneva Conventions. With the specter of the atomic bomb and mass extermination before us, the Geneva Conventions have come to be more than a deal between nations that "if you treat my guys well, I'll treat yours well." Instead, they have become, in the words of Jean de Preux, "a solemn affirmation of principles respected for their own sake."[25] Honoring the Geneva Conventions is the mark of a civilized nation, regardless of what the other side does.

The leaders of Serbia, Bosnia and Herzegovina, and Croatia sign a peace accord in Dayton, Ohio, on November 11, 1995.

FIVE

HUMAN RIGHTS TODAY

The last time his friends saw Manfredo Velásquez Rodríguez, he was walking along the streets of Tegucigalpa, Honduras. That was on September 12, 1981. Rodríguez, a student at a nearby university, was one of thousands of people to disappear during the 1970s and 1980s at the hands of repressive governments in Central and South American countries.

The Inter-American Commission on Human Rights (IA Commission) took Rodríguez's case before the Inter-American Court of Human Rights. The court found evidence that members of the Honduras armed forces had kidnapped Rodríguez, supposedly to gain information about opposition to the government. The young husband and father had been tortured, killed, and secretly buried.[1]

In 1988, in a landmark case, the court ruled that the government of Honduras was responsible for Rodríguez's disappearance and had violated his right to liberty, humane treatment, and life. The court ordered the government to pay damages to Rodríguez's family.[2] Rodríguez's case is just one example of how international organizations are fighting human rights violations.

MORE THAN TWENTY COVENANTS

In the years since the Geneva Conventions of 1949 were adopted, the United Nations has issued more than twenty covenants on women's rights, genocide, racial discrimination, the rights of children, political and civil rights, and social and economic rights, among others.

In drawing up the treaties, however, United Nations delegates have had difficulty resolving wide differences between nations. Democratic nations such as the United States want to emphasize the rights of the individual. Socialist nations such as those in the Communist bloc stress the role of society and the individual's duties to the community. It took the world body until 1966 to draw up two treaties designed to enforce the provisions of the Universal Declaration of Human Rights. The treaties had first been discussed in 1946.

The Covenant on Political and Civil Rights guaranteed the fundamental freedoms outlined in the first twenty-one articles of the Universal Declaration of Human Rights (speech, self-government, religion, and so forth). It didn't go into effect until March 23, 1976, when enough member nations finally ratified it. U.S. President Jimmy Carter, a strong advocate for human rights, signed the treaty on October 5, 1977, but the Senate refused to ratify the pact. Carter's lack of support in Congress and Ronald Reagan's election as president in 1980 sidelined

Jimmy Carter signed the Covenant on Political and Civil Rights and the Covenant on Economic, Social, and Cultural Rights on October 5, 1977, as UN Secretary General Kurt Waldheim watched.

the treaty for fifteen years. Finally, on June 8, 1992, the Senate ratified the treaty after pressure from human rights groups raised public awareness of the issue. The United States became the 104th nation to agree to the treaty's terms.

The second treaty, the Covenant on Economic, Social, and Cultural Rights, went into effect in January 1976. It guaranteed the rights detailed in the second part of the UN declaration (work, social security, education, and so forth). Carter also signed that covenant. President Bill Clinton has expressed support for the treaty, but the U.S. Senate has not yet ratified it. Conservatives have charged that the treaty would force the United States to set up expensive welfare programs, free health care, and other costly services for its citizens.

Other UN covenants have encountered similar resistance from the U.S. Senate and other nations' governments. Although most nations have been willing to sign declarations that support the concept of human rights, few are willing to commit themselves to enforcing human rights. Especially during the Cold War era, countries on both sides did not want to ratify treaties that would expose them to criticism from the enemy. The United States, embroiled in black Americans' civil rights struggle, feared that the Soviet Union would use the Covenant on the Elimination of All Forms of Racial Discrimination as a way of interfering in America's domestic affairs. Although the treaty became effective on January 4, 1969, the U.S. Senate did not ratify it until 1994.

Regional groups have been more effective in winning support for treaties and for enforcing human rights abuses, as in the case of Manfredo Velásquez Rodríguez. Using the UN Declaration and covenants as models, nations in Western Europe, South and Central America, and Africa have adopted their own declarations of human rights, treaties that bind their members to protect those rights, and courts to enforce their provisions.

The Inter-American Commission on Human Rights,

established in 1959, reports on human rights abuses in Latin American countries. It takes violations, like the Honduras case, to the Inter-American Court of Human Rights. In June 1994, the General Assembly of the Organization of American States (the parent of the IA Commission) signed an Inter-American Convention on the Prevention of Forced Disappearances. The convention was designed to end, among OAS nations, the abuses that took the life of Manfredo Rodríguez.

Western European countries founded their own human rights organization in 1950. Its Court of Human Rights has taken strong stands against unlawful detentions and torture in Greece, ruled on violations of free speech and of the press, and challenged unfair treatment of criminals. In 1995, the court took England to task for killing three suspected members of the Irish Republican Army in Gibraltar. The killings, the court ruled, were unnecessary and had violated the dead men's rights.[3]

ADVANCING THE CAUSE

Individual world leaders have also advanced the cause of human rights. U.S. President Gerald Ford and Soviet President Leonid Brezhnev agreed to uphold basic human rights as part of the Helsinki Accords signed in 1975. The Helsinki pact helped focus attention on human rights as an important part of relations between nations.

During his presidency in the late 1970s, Jimmy Carter made human rights a key in his dealings with other countries. He weighed the human rights records of nations— friend and foe—when considering foreign aid requests and pushed for the release of Soviet dissidents. Dissidents take public stands against their governments' policies. Often, they are imprisoned or tortured for their views.

In the 1980s, Soviet leader Mikhail Gorbachev brought human rights reform to his country, and in 1991, the Soviet Union hosted a UN Human Rights Conference.

At the invitation of U.S. President Bill Clinton, the presidents of the Republic of Serbia, Bosnia and govina, and Croatia met on November 1, 1995, at the Wright-Patterson Air Force Base in Dayton, Ohio, to negotiate a settlement to a three-year war in the former Yugoslavia. Three weeks later, Serb President Slobodan Milosevic, Bosnian President Alija Izetbegovic, and Croatian president Franjo Tudjman initialed a peace treaty. The Dayton Peace Accord established Bosnia as an independent state with free elections. Under the treaty terms, Bosnia was divided into two parts, one under the control of the Muslim-Croat federation and one controlled by Bosnian Serbs. The peace accord was formally signed on December 14, 1995, in Paris.

The bitter war erupted in April 1992 when the Muslim government of Bosnia decided to secede from Yugoslavia, controlled by Serbs. Bosnian Serbs, opposed to the secession and backed by Yugoslavia, marshaled troops against their Muslim neighbors. Croatia later sided with Bosnian Muslims against the Serbs. In the brutal fighting that followed, forty thousand to fifty thousand people died, and the homes of two million to three million were destroyed. More than two million refugees fled Bosnia.

During the war, UN officials documented many hu-

The Dayton Peace Accord divided Bosnia into two parts, one controlled by the Muslim-Croat federation and the other by the Serbs.

man rights abuses, including rapes, executions, and attacks on declared safe areas. There were also reports of mass executions in an effort by Serbs to eliminate their Muslim neighbors. This policy of mass slaughter was called ethnic cleansing. Reports of such atrocities at Srebrenica, on the Serbian-Bosnian border, and elsewhere finally led the United States to push the warring nations to negotiate a settlement.

ENFORCEMENT EFFORTS

Enforcement continues to be a weak spot in international human rights efforts. On May 30, 1992, the UN Security council imposed tough sanctions, including a trade embargo and a freeze on Serbian assets in foreign banks, against the Serbs in Yugoslavia. North Atlantic Treaty Organization (NATO) forces conducted air strikes against Serbs in Bosnia. Both efforts helped bring the parties to the negotiating table but not before millions were killed and massive human rights violations were committed. The Dayton Peace Accord called for an international board to oversee elections in Bosnia and to protect the human rights of the Bosnian people. NATO forces—including a large contingent from the United States—were to enforce the agreement.

In Rwanda, a 1994 uprising resulted in "the worst genocide and mass slaughter Africa had ever seen."[4] The battle for control of the government pitted the Hutus, who made up a majority of the population, against the Tutsi. In the ensuing civil war, which also engulfed Burundi, Hutu soldiers massacred at least one million Tutsi and their more moderate Hutu supporters. The overthrow of the radical Hutu regime by Tutsi leaders ended the massacres, but tensions between the two groups remained high. Tutsi seeking revenge attacked Hutus in Rwanda and at refugee camps outside the country. The UN Security Council agreed to send soldiers to help protect refugees and human rights workers administering aid in the war-torn region, but the United States and other nations—discouraged by similar efforts in Bosnia and Somalia—were reluctant to send more troops to troubled areas. France eventually agreed to send forces to back the UN peace-seeking mission.

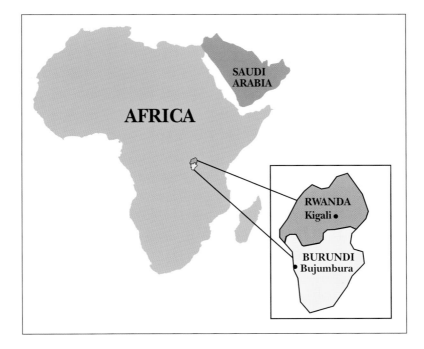

In 1994, Rwanda and Burundi were engulfed in a brutal civil war between the ruling Tutsi and the majority Hutus.

International pressure has had only limited success in easing human rights abuses in China. In August 1995, China released U.S. human rights activist Harry Wu, who had been sentenced to fifteen years in jail, after worldwide protests that threatened to mar China's hosting of the UN Conference on Women. But in December, Chinese dissident Wei Jingsheng was sentenced to fourteen years in prison for criticizing the government. Another dissident, Wang Dan, received an eleven-year sentence for sedition in November 1996 after a closed, four-hour trial. Despite criticism from the United States and elsewhere, Chinese leaders have resisted outside demands to improve its record on human rights, insisting that China must "determine its own path."[5]

A number of UN-run agencies deal with abuses of human rights. The UN Human Rights Commission meets six weeks a year to hear complaints from nations and individuals. It then determines whether human rights abuses have been committed. Though the commission has no enforcement power, it ranks the severity of each case. Nations receiving a poor rating on human rights can lose foreign aid and loans and be subject to other sanctions.

The International Court of Justice, located at The Hague, rules on disputes between nations. Both nations in question, however, have to agree before a case can be taken to the court of justice.

In 1993, the UN Security Council set up the International Tribunal for the Prosecution of War Crimes to try people accused of human rights atrocities during the war in the former Yugoslavian countries and in Rwanda. It was the first such court established since the Nuremberg Trials, which prosecuted Nazi war criminals after World War II. Those found guilty of war crimes could face long prison terms.

Groups of nations also use sanctions to enforce human rights violations. Countries throughout the world stopped trade and diplomatic relations with South Africa during the 1980s and early 1990s to force an end to that nation's racial discrimination policies.

Several nations have passed laws based on the provisions of the human rights treaties they have signed. Those laws can sometimes help protect citizens from human rights abuses.

Private human rights groups use other techniques, such as shaming violators or media attention, to fight hu-

A UN soldier from Australia carries a Hutu orphan to safety after the child's mother was killed in a massacre at the Kibeho refugee camp in southwestern Rwanda on April 22, 1996. The United Nations estimated two thousand Hutu refugees were killed by revenge-seeking Tutsi in the massacre.

man rights abuses. Amnesty International, founded by British lawyer Peter Benenson in 1960, has been a leading force against the use of torture. Group members publicize human rights abuses by telling the media about individual cases, investigating reports of abuse, and issuing statements on their findings. The group's worldwide membership writes letters to government leaders and others to win the release of political prisoners. Because they are not associated with any nation or political party, the private groups are often more believable than governmental bodies.

Henri Dunant, awarded the Nobel Peace Prize in 1901 for his work for the humane treatment of wounded soldiers, knew that war leads to human rights abuses. Almost a century later, at the UN World Conference on Human Rights in Vienna in 1993, Dunant's fellow Nobel Peace prizewinners noted that the reverse is also true: Human rights abuses lead to war.

In a statement issued at the conference, the peace advocates outlined why the push for human rights is so important to the world:

> One of the fundamental lessons of our time is that respect for human rights is essential for peace. . . . Ethnic wars, growing militarism, racial, religious, cultural and ideological hostility, and the denial of social justice will come to an end if all individuals are brought up, educated and trained in a spirit of tolerance based on respect for human rights.[6]

Convention for the Amelioration of the Condition of the Wounded in Armies in the Field, signed Geneva, August 22, 1864

Article 1

Ambulances and military hospitals shall be recognized as neutral, and as such, protected and respected by the belligerents as long as they accommodate wounded and sick.

Neutrality shall end if the said ambulances or hospitals should be held by a military force.

Article 2

Hospital and ambulance personnel, including the quarter-master's staff, the medical, administrative and transport services, and the chaplains, shall have the benefit of the same neutrality when on duty, and while there remain any wounded to be brought in or assisted.

Article 3

The persons designated in the preceding Article may, even after enemy occupation, continue to discharge their functions in the hospital or ambulance with which they serve, or may withdraw to rejoin the units to which they belong.

When in these circumstances they cease from their functions, such persons shall be delivered to the enemy outposts by the occupying forces.

Article 4

The material of military hospitals being subject to the laws of war, the persons attached to such hospitals may take with them, on withdrawing, only the articles which are their own personal property.

Ambulances, on the contrary, under similar circumstances, shall retain their equipment.

Article 5

Inhabitants of the country who bring help to the wounded shall be respected and shall remain free. Generals of the belligerent Powers shall make it their duty to notify the inhabitants of the appeal made to their humanity, and of the neutrality which humane conduct will confer.

The presence of any wounded combatant receiving shelter and care in a house shall ensure its protection. An inhabitant who has given shelter to the wounded shall be exempted from billeting and from a portion of such war contributions as may be levied.

Article 6

Wounded or sick combatants, to whatever nation they may belong, shall be collected and cared for.

Commanders-in-Chief may hand over immediately to the enemy outposts enemy combatants wounded during an engagement, when circumstances allow and subject to the agreement of both parties.

Those who, after their recovery, are recognized as being unfit for further service, shall be repatriated.

The others may likewise be sent back, on condition

that they shall not again, for the duration of hostilities, take up arms.

Evacuation parties, and the personnel conducting them, shall be considered as being absolutely neutral.

ARTICLE 7

A distinctive and uniform flag shall be adopted for hospitals, ambulances and evacuation parties. It should in all circumstances be accompanied by the national flag.

An armlet may also be worn by personnel enjoying neutrality but its issue shall be left to the military authorities.

Both flag and armlet shall bear a red cross on a white ground.

ARTICLE 8

The implementing of the present Convention shall be arranged by the Commanders-in-Chief of the belligerent armies following the instructions of their respective Governments and in accordance with the general principles set forth in this Convention.

ARTICLE 9

The High Contracting Parties have agreed to communicate the present Convention with an invitation to accede thereto to Governments unable to appoint Plenipotentiaries to the International Conference at Geneva. The Protocol has accordingly been left open.

ARTICLE 10

The present Convention shall be ratified and the ratifications exchanged at Berne, within the next four months, or sooner if possible.

In faith, whereof, the respective Plenipotentiaries have signed the Convention and thereto affixed their seals.

UNIVERSAL DECLARATION OF HUMAN RIGHTS

WHEREAS recognition of the inherent dignity and of the equal and inalienable rights of all members of the human family is the foundation of freedom, justice and peace in the world,

WHEREAS disregard and contempt for human rights have resulted in barbarous acts which have outraged the conscience of mankind, and the advent of a world in which human beings shall enjoy freedom of speech and belief and freedom from fear and want has been proclaimed as the highest aspiration of the common people,

WHEREAS it is essential, if man is not to be compelled to have recourse, as a last resort, to rebellion against tyranny and oppression, that human rights should be protected by the rule of law,

WHEREAS it is essential to promote the development of friendly relations between nations,

WHEREAS the peoples of the United Nations have in their Charter reaffirmed their faith in fundamental human rights, in the dignity and worth of the human person and in the equal rights of men and women and have determined to promote social progress and better standards of life in larger freedom,

WHEREAS Member States have pledged themselves

to achieve, in co-operation with the United Nations, the promotion of universal respect for and observance of human rights and fundamental freedoms,

WHEREAS a common understanding of these rights and freedoms is of the greatest importance for the full realization of this pledge,

NOW, THEREFORE, THE GENERAL ASSEMBLY PROCLAIMS this Universal Declaration of Human Rights as a common standard of achievement for all peoples and all nations, to the end that every individual and every organ of society, keeping this Declaration constantly in mind, shall strive by teaching and education to promote respect for these rights and freedoms and by progressive measures, national and international, to secure their universal and effective recognition and observance, both among the peoples of Members States themselves and among the peoples of territories under their jurisdiction.

ARTICLE 1
All human beings are born free and equal in dignity and rights. They are endowed with reason and conscience and should act towards one another in a spirit of brotherhood.

ARTICLE 2
Everyone is entitled to all the rights and freedoms set forth in this Declaration, without distinction of any kind, such as race, colour, sex, language, religion, political or

other opinion, national or social origin, property, birth or other status. Furthermore, no distinction shall be made on the basis of the political, jurisdictional or international status of the country or territory to which a person belongs, whether it be independent, trust, non-self-governing or under any other limitation of sovereignty.

ARTICLE 3

Everyone has the right to life, liberty and security of person.

ARTICLE 4

No one shall be held in slavery or servitude; slavery and the slave trade shall be prohibited in all their forms.

ARTICLE 5

No one shall be subjected to torture or to cruel, inhuman or degrading treatment or punishment.

ARTICLE 6

Everyone has the right to recognition everywhere as a person before the law.

ARTICLE 7

All are equal before the law and are entitled without discrimination to equal protection of the law. All are entitled to equal protection against any discrimination in violation of this Declaration and against any incitement to such discrimination.

ARTICLE 8

Everyone has the right to an effective remedy by the competent national tribunals for acts violating the fundamental rights granted him by the constitution or by law.

ARTICLE 9

No one shall be subjected to arbitrary arrest, detention or exile.

ARTICLE 10

Everyone is entitled in full equality to a fair and public hearing by an independent and impartial tribunal, in the determination of his rights and obligations and of any criminal charge against him.

ARTICLE 11

(1) Everyone charged with a penal offence has the right to be presumed innocent until proved guilty according to law in a public trial at which he has had all the guarantees necessary for his defence.

(2) No one shall be held guilty of any penal offence on account of any act or omission which did not constitute a penal offence, under national or international law, at the time when it was committee. Nor shall a heavier penalty be imposed than the one that was applicable at the time the penal offence was committed.

ARTICLE 12

No one shall be subjected to arbitrary interference with his privacy, family, home or correspondence, nor to attacks upon his honour and reputation. Everyone has the right to the protection of the law against such inter-ference or attacks.

ARTICLE 13

(1) Everyone has the right to freedom of movement and residence within the borders of each state.

(2) Everyone has the right to leave any country, in-cluding his own, and to return to his country.

ARTICLE 14

(1) Everyone has the right to seek and to enjoy in oth-er countries asylum from persecution.

(2) This right may not be invoked in the case of pros-ecutions genuinely arising from non-political crimes or from acts contrary to the purposes and principles of the United Nations.

ARTICLE 15

(1) Everyone has the right to a nationality.

(2) No one shall be arbitrarily deprived of his nation-ality nor denied the right to change his nationality.

ARTICLE 16

(1) Men and women of full age, without any limita-tion due to race, nationality or religion, have the right to marry and to found a family. They are entitled to equal rights as to marriage, during marriage and at its dissolu-tion.

(2) Marriage shall be entered into only with the free and full consent of the intending spouses.

(3) The family is the natural and fundamental group

unit of society and is entitled to protection by society and the State.

ARTICLE 17

(1) Everyone has the right to own property alone as well as in association with others.

(2) No one shall be arbitrarily deprived of his property.

ARTICLE 18

Everyone has the right to freedom of thought, conscience and religion; this right includes freedom to change his religion or belief, and freedom, either alone or in community with others and in public or private, to manifest his religion or belief in teaching, practice, worship and observance.

ARTICLE 19

Everyone has the right to freedom of opinion and expression; this right includes freedom to hold opinions without interference and to seek, receive and impart information and ideas through any media and regardless of frontiers.

ARTICLE 20

(1) Everyone has the right to freedom of peaceful assembly and association.

(2) No one may be compelled to belong to an association.

Article 21

(1) Everyone has the right to take part in the government of his country, directly or through freely chosen representatives.

(2) Everyone has the right of equal access to public service in his country.

(3) The will of the people shall be the basis of the authority of government; this will shall be expressed in periodic and genuine elections which shall be by universal and equal suffrage and shall be held by secret vote or by equivalent free voting procedures.

Article 22

Everyone, as a member of society, has the right to social security and is entitled to realization, through national effort and international cooperation and in accordance with the organization and resources of each State, of the economic, social and cultural rights indispensable for his dignity and the free development of his personality.

Article 23

(1) Everyone has the right to work, to free choice of employment, to just and favourable conditions of work and to protection against unemployment.

(2) Everyone, without any discrimination, has the right to equal pay for equal work.

(3) Everyone who works has the right to just and favourable remuneration ensuring for himself and his family an existence worthy of human dignity, and supplement, if necessary, by other means of social protection.

(4) Everyone has the right to form and to join trade unions for the protection of his interests.

Article 24

Everyone has the right to rest and leisure, including reasonable limitation of working hours and periodic holidays with pay.

Article 25

(1) Everyone has the right to a standard of living adequate for the health and well-being of himself and of his family, including food, clothing, housing and medical care and necessary social services, and the right to security in the event of unemployment, sickness, disability, widowhood, old age or other lack of livelihood in circumstances beyond his control.

(2) Motherhood and childhood are entitled to special care and assistance. All children, whether born in or out of wedlock, shall enjoy the same social protection.

Article 26

(1) Everyone has the right to education. Education shall be free, at least in the elementary and fundamental stages. Elementary education shall be compulsory. Technical and professional education shall be made generally available and higher education shall be equally accessible to all on the basis of merit.

(2) Education shall be directed to the full development of the human personality and to the strengthening of respect for human rights and fundamental freedoms. It shall promote understanding, tolerance and friendship

among all nations, racial or religious groups, and shall further the activities of the United Nations for the maintenance of peace.

(3) Parents have a prior right to choose the kind of education that shall be given to their children.

ARTICLE 27

(1) Everyone has the right freely to participate in the cultural life of the community, to enjoy the arts and to share in scientific advancement and its benefits.

(2) Everyone has the right to the protection of the moral and material interests resulting from any scientific, literary or artistic production of which he is the author.

ARTICLE 28

Everyone is entitled to a social and international order in which the rights and freedoms set forth in this Declaration can be fully realized.

ARTICLE 29

(1) Everyone has duties to the community in which alone the free and full development of his personality is possible.

(2) In the exercise of his rights and freedoms, everyone shall be subject only to such limitations as are determined by law solely for the purpose of securing due recognition and respect for the rights and freedoms of others and of meeting the just requirements of morality, public order and the general welfare in a democratic society.

(3) These rights and freedoms may in no case be ex-

ercises contrary to the purposes and principles of the United Nations.

ARTICLE 30

Nothing in this Declaration may be interpreted as implying for any State, group or person any right to engage in any activity or to perform any act aimed at the destruction of any of the rights and freedoms set forth herein.

Source Notes

INTRODUCTION

1. Schindler, Dietrich, and Jirí Toman, eds., *The Laws of Armed Conflicts: A Collection of Conventions, Resolutions and Other Documents* (Rockville, Md.: Sijthoff & Noordhoff, 1981), p. 197.

2. Dunant, J. Henri, *A Memory of Solferino* (Washington, D.C.: The American National Red Cross, 1959), p. 84.

3. Lash, Joseph P. *Eleanor: The Years Alone* (New York: W. W. Norton, 1972), p. 79.

4. Ibid.

CHAPTER ONE

1. Dunant, p. 9. The description of the Battle of Solferino is based on Dunant's memoir.

2. Ibid.

3. Ibid.

4. Ibid., p. 33.

5. Ibid., p. 35.

6. Ibid., p. 38

7. Ibid.

8. Dunant, p. 32.

9. Downey, Fairfax, *Disaster Fighters* (New York: G. P. Putnam's Sons, 1938), p. 17.

10. Schindler, p. 6. ("Instructions for the Government of Armies of the United States in the Field," Section I: Art. 15.)

11. Ibid., p. 18. ("Instructions for the Government of Armies of the United States in the Field," Section VI: Art. 115.)

12. Downey, p. 22.

13. Ibid., p. 23.

14. Pictet, Jean. *Development and Principles of International Humanitarian Law* (Boston: Martinus Nijhoff Publishers, 1985), p. 31.

15. Schindler, p. 32. (Brussels Conference 1874, Art. 38.)

16. Ibid., p. 49.

17. Ibid., p. 235. (Geneva Convention 1906, Chapter I: Art. 5.)

18. Ibid., p. 214. (Geneva Convention 1864, Chapter I: Art. 5.)

CHAPTER TWO

1. Dunant, p. 73.

2. Smith, Page, *America Enters the World: A People's History of the Progressive Era and World War I,* vol. 7 (New York: McGraw-Hill, 1985), p. 460.

3. Ibid., p. 464.

4. Ibid.

5. Ibid., p. 699.

6. Ibid., pp. 707–708.

7. Stokesbury, James L., *A Short History of World War I* (New York: William Morrow, 1981), p. 322.

8. Schindler, p. 273. (Geneva Convention 1929, preamble.)

9. Herczegh, Géza, *Development of International Humanitarian Law* (Budapest: Akadémiai Kiadó, 1984), p. 19.

10. Ibid., p. 42.

11. Schindler, p. 427.

CHAPTER THREE
1. Goodwin, Doris Kearns, *No Ordinary Time* (New York: Simon & Schuster, 1994), p. 151.
2. Ibid., p. 152.
3. Smith, p. 718.
4. Goodwin, p. 621.
5. Ibid., p. 619.
6. Henkin, Louis, *The Rights of Man Today* (Boulder, Col.: Westview Press, 1978), p. 93.
7. Lash, pp. 35–36.

CHAPTER FOUR
1. Lash, p. 45.
2. Ibid., p. 48.
3. Ibid., pp. 53–54.
4. Ibid.
5. Ibid.
6. Ibid., p. 66.
7. Ibid., p. 71.
8. Ibid.
9. Ibid., p. 78.
10. Ibid., p. 80.
11. Pictet, p. 37.
12. de Preux, Jean, *Commentary: III Geneva Convention Relative to the Treatment of Prisoners of War* (Geneva: International Committee of the Red Cross, 1960), p. 4.
13. Ibid., p. 9.
14. Ibid., p. 8.
15. Ibid., p. 23.

16. Ibid., p. 140.

17. Schindler, p. 442. (Fourth Geneva Convention 1949, Part III: Section I: Art. 27.)

18. Herczegh, p. 93.

19. Dunant, p. 83.

20. Herczegh, p. 55 *note.*

21. de Preux, p. 140.

22. Ibid., p. 627.

23. Ibid., p. 10.

24. Ibid.

25. Ibid., p. 20.

CHAPTER FIVE

1. Abi-Mershed, Elizabeth, "Thirty-five Years Defending Human Rights," *Américas,* vol. 46, no. 6 (November–December 1994), p. 51–52.

2. Ibid., p. 52.

3. Fitzgerald, Patrick, "Tories Rattled by Gibraltar Verdict," *New Statesman & Society,* vol. 8, no. 373 (October 6, 1995), pp. 7–8.

4. *1995 Compton's Year Book* (Chicago: Compton's Learning Co., 1995), p. 323.

5. *1995 Compton's Year Book* (Chicago: Compton's Learning Co., 1995), p. 189.

6. Mock, Alois. "A New Departure," *UNESCO Courier* (March 1994), p. 38.

OTHER REFERENCES

Annual Report of the Inter-American Commission on Human Rights 1994. Washington, D.C.: Organization of American States, 1995.

Fast, Howard, ed. *The Selected Work of Tom Paine.* New York: Duell, Sloan and Pearce, 1945.

Larson, Egon. *A Flame in Barbed Wire: The Story of Amnesty International.* New York: W. W. Norton, 1979.

Wolfgang, Marvin E., ed. *The Annals of The American Academy of Political and Social Science, Human Rights Around the World.* Newbury Park, Calif.: Sage Publications, 1989.

Bliven, Bruce. *From Casablanca to Berlin.* New York: Random House, 1965.

Bowen, R. S. *They Flew to Glory.* New York: Lothrop, 1965.

Brimner, Larry Dane. *Voices from the Camps: Internment of Japanese Americans During World War II.* Danbury, Conn.: Franklin Watts, 1994.

Bronson, Marsha. *Amnesty International: Organizations That Help the World.* Parsippany, N.J.: Silver Burdett, 1994.

Cannon, Marian G. *Dwight David Eisenhower: War Hero and President.* Danbury, Conn.: Franklin Watts, 1990.

Caulkins, Janet. *Joseph Stalin.* Danbury, Conn.: Franklin Watts, 1990.

Dunant, Henri. *A Memory of Solferino.* Washington, D.C.: The American National Red Cross, 1959.

Dunnahoo, Terry. *Pearl Harbor: America Enters the War.* Danbury, Conn.: Franklin Watts, 1991.

Feinberg, Barbara Silberdick. *Harry S. Truman.* Danbury, Conn.: Franklin Watts, 1994.

Frankel, Marvin E., and Ellen Saideman. *Out of the Shadows of Night: The Struggle for International Human Rights.* New York: Delacorte Press, 1989.

Goodwin, Doris Kearns. *No Ordinary Time.* New York: Simon & Schuster, 1994.

Greenberg, Judith E., and Helen Carey McKeever, *Letters From a World War II GI.* Danbury, Conn.: Franklin Watts, 1995.

Hacker, Jeffrey. *Franklin D. Roosevelt*. New York: Benchmark Books, 1991.

Handler, Andrew, and Susan V. Meschel. *Young People Speak: Surviving the Holocaust in Hungary*. Danbury, Conn.: Franklin Watts, 1993.

Hoobler, Dorothy, and Thomas Hoobler. *Mandela: The Man, the Struggle, the Triumph*. Danbury, Conn.: Franklin Watts, 1992.

Jacobs, William J. *Eleanor Roosevelt: A Life of Happiness and Tears*. New York: Benchmark Books, 1991.

Johnson, Edward. *United Nations: Peacekeeper*. New York: Thomson Learning, 1995.

Kronenwetter, Michael. *Taking a Stand Against Human Rights Abuses*. Danbury, Conn.: Franklin Watts, 1990.

Kuklin, Susan. *Irrepressible Spirit: Conversations With Human Rights Activists*. New York: Putnam, 1996.

Landau, Elaine. *We Survived the Holocaust*. Danbury, Conn.: Franklin Watts, 1991.

Larsen, Rebecca. *Franklin D. Roosevelt: Man of Destiny*. Danbury, Conn.: Franklin Watts, 1991.

Lash, Joseph P. *Eleanor: The Years Alone*. New York: W. W. Norton & Co., 1972.

Peck, Rodney. *Working Together Against Human Rights Violations*. New York: Rosen Publishing Group, 1994.

Pollard, Michael. *United Nations: Organizations That Help the World*. Parsippany, N.J.: Silver Burdett, 1995.

Sherwin, Jane. *Human Rights*. Vero Beach, Fla.: Rourke Corp., 1990.

Smith, Page. *America Enters the World: A People's History of the Progressive Era and World War I*, Vol. 7. New York: McGraw-Hill, 1985.

Spencer, William. *Germany Then and Now.* Danbury, Conn.: Franklin Watts, 1994.

Sulzberger, C. L. *The American Heritage Picture History of World War II.* New York: Simon & Schuster, 1966.

Toland, John. *The Last 100 Days.* New York: Random House, 1966.

Ushan, Michael V. *Multicultural Portrait of World War I.* New York: Benchmark Books, 1996.

Vaughan, Edwin Campion. *Some Desperate Glory: The World War I Diary of a British Officer, 1917.* New York: Henry Holt, 1981.

Wright, David K. *Multicultural Portrait of World War II.* New York: Benchmark Books, 1996.

INDEX